# Beyond
## Healing

Messages our loved ones, angels, and
guides want us to hear

*Debbie:*
*Love on this*
*amazing journey*
*Hugs*
*Laurie*

L a u r i e   W o n d r a

# Contents

# Acknowledgments

In writing this book, the content and flow came through me within a matter of a few months. I knew at that time that the content of this book had great purpose, and messages and information were being pushed from somewhere beyond—and from something greater than me. To this day, as I look back over that time in my life, I know there was a divine timing, and a greater energy. In other words, more hands, minds, and ideas, and definitely more energy, were involved in this project than simply mine.

It was also a perfect time in my life to focus on writing. I had left one job where I routinely traveled for business and taken a position that allowed me to be at home with my children, and to focus on my family and friends, as well as a growing list of people seeking my help to speak to their loved ones, or to their angels and guides. There was a persistent yearning in my soul, and with each person I worked with, that calling was pushed deeper. Whether planned or not, my life was changing, and with my first book, I'd sent a message to the universe that I was ready to grow and expand. It felt like I had suddenly waved a *huge* white flag and was surrendering to the universe. I would stop hiding, and announce my gift and the use of it to the world.

Once I began the writing process by defining an outline, the information, stories, events, and clarity all came in a timely manner. There was no way to slow this flow of information. In some cases, I would stay up writing late into the night, and spirit would download information or flash memories into my mind, and through my hands the words would appear on paper. I sent the first few chapters to my dear friend and mentor, Anita Cassidy. She was my greatest cheerleader and confidante during my first book, and now with *Beyond Healing*. Having written five books, Anita's coaching was pivotal to the editing, with her solid recommendations for clarity and suggestions for changes. Her encouragement and excitement for this material greatly helped in getting it to the point of completion. I have deep gratitude for her contributions to the end result.

Those that read the early chapters were also great cheerleaders. I am immensely grateful for their input, and for urging me to keep writing and to get it published. They understood that there were messages and information that needed to be shared, aside from the human interest. Many who contributed are curious about the afterlife, and most had their own experiences with loved ones, angels, or guides. All I have listed here are very important for the stories they shared, or for the times they allowed me into their lives, and then to write about their experiences. Many blessings to Paulette, Jill, Judy, Linda, Leslie, and Debra for sharing your experiences with me, and continuing with your curiosity to go beyond by expanding your fields of energy. Thank you, Eva, Lee and Stephanie for your continued belief in me and my work, and for sharing your experiences. You are a blessing to many. Thanks to Sandy and Carolyn, for spending extra time with me in sharing your experiences and allowing me the honor of being a conduit for you and your loved ones. I will always be touched and grateful for these connections. And to my dear childhood friends, Kathy and Mecque, who have known me *forever*, thank you for your common sense and unwavering faith in my gifts. You were the very first to trust me with the caring words from your loved ones that made us both believe that they never leave us; they only move on to a different type of energy.

Thank you to Connie Anderson, for her editing and direction that kept me grounded in words that sometimes I just assumed were common terms for all. It was during this stage that I heard from the angels: "We are now done please publish."

To my daughter Emma who utilized her amazing ability with photography to create the pictures and the art images that then became the final cover design. Who knew that when you took those pictures they would become this cover.

To my cover designer Alan Pranke who recreated the cover based on an idea and images provided. Thank you for your eye for refinement and subtle changes that were important to me to create the final image and the overall look of the book.

To my children, Jake and Emma, who have been so accepting of living in a supercharged energy-based home and who sometimes have no choice but to experience my life and the visitors that seek me out. Your love and ability to openly trust are an inspiration to me and to those around us. I am blessed to have both of you in my life while we travel our personal journeys, as well as this journey as a family. I love each of you very dearly. To my parents, both of this earth and beyond, that continue to teach from both sides of the veil. Thank you.

I remain eternally grateful to all the angels, guides, and loved ones that contributed to the content of this book, and to all the loving beings that surround me each and every day. I feel forever blessed with each loving interaction. Your protection, honesty, intellect, and love are truly gifts for every person you interact with. Though it is me that people physically see, it is you that do all the work.

# Introduction

The best part of using my gift is when I can help people make connections. When I speak of making a connection, it is through a conversation or knowledge that is provided to a client from guides and angelic beings, or light beings. It could also be a conversation with a loved one that has died. My clients quite frequently ask about the difference between guides, angelic beings, light beings, and the energy from loved ones that have passed. They are all loving beings that are around us to help us on our journey. They are available to guide and direct, and to answer our questions. They speak to us in words, symbols, and other methods of information that are available if we are aware, alert, and open to receiving these messages. Sometimes our logical brains reason away these messages. We become locked into analytic information that has a scientific foundation, rather than a mystical one.

While I was growing up, psychics, healers, astrologers, palm readers, and channelers all intrigued me, and every few years I would work up the courage to make an appointment and actually see one face-to-face. I was frequently told that I was very intuitive, and would be a healer; probably working with those that had crossed over. I felt I was intuitive, and I often would know things that others around me did not know. Information would seemingly pop into my head, and where it had come from, I couldn't actually pinpoint.

## Trip to Mexico

One such time was on a women's vacation with fifteen of my friends. For this trip we chose Mazatlan, Mexico, as a destination. Like most twenty-one-year-olds at that time, we spent our days on the beach and our evenings dancing. I have never been one to stay in one spot for long, preferring to see the sights and go for walks. A few days into the trip, I got overly hot and was tired of just lying around, so I wandered into a nearby hotel. This was not the hotel where we were staying. For whatever reason, that day I wandered into the lobby of this particular hotel.

A woman was doing psychic readings, and on impulse, I signed up for a private reading. When my scheduled time arrived, she was nowhere to be found, but I waited patiently. She arrived fifteen minutes later and apologized profusely. As I listened to her, a calm, flowing, warm energy moved over the top of us. In mid-sentence, she stopped and said, "Thank you." Her thank-you was based on the healing energy she felt move down through her body. She felt I had assisted with this warm energy she was feeling as it moved through her body, settling in her abdomen. She had not been feeling well all morning, and had stopped at her doctor's office to see if he could explain her stomach pains. He couldn't to her satisfaction, and simply sent her on her way, saying it was cramps or a simple stomachache. I had sensed it was something else, and as she thanked me for making her feel better, words were flowing from my mouth. I told her that she should listen to her mother, who kept telling her that she was not done with these stomach pains, and she would eventually undergo some surgery that would make her feel much better.

I sat back in the chair, not totally comprehending where the words were coming from; they were just there. It somehow felt as if they had manifested in my head from someplace beyond this earth. Then, she said she knew exactly what I was talking about, but was afraid to push the doctor for further testing, and had not been totally honest with him about her symptoms. She said that her mother had died a number of years ago, and often spoke to her, particularly when she needed additional help with something. She again thanked me for bringing the energy in, and for the clarity on what she needed to do. We talked for a bit, and she told me I did not need a reading, as I was an old soul with many lifetimes as a healer—and I already knew that, I just needed to wake up to my gifts and how to help people. She also thanked me for making the connection with her mom. She said she would now take the necessary medical steps without carrying the fear she had been feeling.

## Denying My Gifts

I liked hearing that I had an intuitive gift, but at age twenty-one, I did not like hearing that I'd be using it to speak to dead people. Of course, I had not made the connection that helping people speak to their deceased loved ones would be a healing in itself. I'd be helping people get a healing from beyond; not in the sense of a physical healing, but a healing of emotional turmoil, or a completion to some unfinished event—a healing of energy.

For years, I denied use of this gift, thinking that to open the door would be like opening a door to the dark side, and it scared me. I had grown up watching too many bad horror movies, and had read too many books that did not explain energy in the sense of what is known today. I chose to live my life optimistically looking forward, as I felt it matched my optimist personal outlook on life. Looking to the future meant never looking back with regret or turmoil. No one could change anything in the past, so why linger there? My motto was to learn from each opportunity, make appropriate changes, and then move forward. It is much more fun to look ahead for those happy, shiny moments. I now realize how deeply seated our lives can be in past or unfinished events, which sometimes require us to look back in order to move forward.

## Sondra's Visitor

The universe has a way of continuing to push us to use our gifts when we are supposed to, and if we ignore them, they have a way of just showing up. Over ten years ago, this happened at work with my then administrative assistant. Sondra was extremely efficient, and she would often walk into my office to see if I needed anything. Most of the time it was to remind me to take a break. Each time she entered, an elderly white-haired gentleman would follow her. I could make out a few general features, but nothing in great detail. I did know he was a father or grandfather. For months, this man would follow Sondra around, urging me to speak about his presence. I hesitated because Sondra did not know I had this gift, and broaching this subject felt uncomfortable. I had no way of knowing if Sondra believed in psychics or intuitive readers. As the weeks went by, I realized this gentleman was not going to leave me alone until I at least told her about what I was seeing. He wanted to talk to her and let her know he was there, whispering in her ear. I began by talking about my own father, to whom I am very close, and how he had a habit of calling each of his children every weekend. If he ever missed one of us, our weekend seemed off balance in an odd way. With that opening, I could not hold back his messages. "Sondra, your father is here, and he wants you to know that he is standing alongside you right now, whispering in your ear that everything is going to be all right, and that you are doing the right things to care for your mom." He was there on the other side, helping, but he wanted Sondra to be strong and to know there was no more that she could do. As soon as I'd said the words, he was gone, satisfied that his message had been delivered. Over time I got to know Sondra's father quite well. Some days I would find him standing in my office, waiting; other times he'd follow her into my office, and would begin by sending huge hugs to his daughter. When her mother became ill, Sondra found comfort in her father's words. Sondra and I remain connected, and we both have this wonderful memory of my introduction to her father.

In time, I learned ways to tune out these energies so that I could continue with my office work. This allowed me to have a choice of when to communicate with these energies, so when I did, they had my full attention. Now the door was open.

It took a number of years for me to go public. I had the lingering fear of being judged, and worried about what people would think. I certainly did not want to be considered weird. Already I had collected all sorts of ungrounded fears. Finally, my gifts could not be hidden any longer. There was a longing within me to be of service to people. I didn't see how I could continue to remain in an executive management position of my information technology profession while also exploring my gifts publicly. I did, however, know that it was my purpose to use these gifts and the messages from beyond to bring information and knowledge to this earthly dimension. I had the faith that I would be provided the information needed to continue in a corporate position while using my spiritual gifts. I have been very blessed with lifelong friends and reconnections to friends who are just as curious as I am. Also, an awakening process is moving through this plane of existence, pushing people to search for answers, purpose, and direction. It is because of this curiousness, in addition to the desire of so many people to step into their own calling, that I literally have been pushed by the universe to act upon my gifts, well beyond what was once my comfort zone. That zone seems to expand to mirror the expansion of my gifts. I am more in tune with my purpose and receive more loving support here on earth than ever before. With this earthly support comes the flood of help from the guides, angelic beings, and our loved ones that have crossed over. This trust, and being surrounded by all this love and compassion, pushes me to such gratitude as I am asked to pass along these messages and information.

We are all lifelong learners, and the education we receive is not only in a classroom and from a formal curriculum. Our entire universe is our classroom. If we open our minds to receive, we are able to tap into information that is beyond the physical presence of a book or material that we can touch with our hands and see with our eyes. If we open our senses and mind, information from beyond this dimension is available to us.

Our loved ones, our angels and guides, are ready to give us knowledge and other information. They are aware of the importance of closure, and sometimes this means providing answers to questions that were left unanswered during their time here on earth. In this book are real-life stories of readings I have done with clients and family, along with my own personal experiences. They are teaching episodes that help us understand what our loved ones experience during and after they have crossed over. They are stories of affirmation that our loved ones continue to remain connected with us, and that the angelic beings, guides, and light beings have a desire to help us on our journey. We are all moving along this common path that we call living on earth, but all does not stop there.

In the following chapters, I write about their messages and the information they want many of us to know and hear. All the stories are true, but the names of the clients and their loved ones have been changed, unless the client directed me to use real names. I appreciate each client and love every encounter. I remain deeply grateful to all those that I have worked with, and for the trust and faith they have put in me—and my gifts. I also have much gratitude for the angelic beings, and for the family members that come forward to reconnect with those still here on earth. I am truly blessed.

# Chapter 1

# Making A Connection; Is It Real?

Once I began doing public readings for clients, the connections were with guides, angels, and light-energy beings—not with loved ones that had crossed over. I now believe that those connections had been available to me since I was a child, but I chose not to focus there when I worked with clients. Rather, I would work with a client's angels or guides. I would, however, connect often with my grandma, and feel her loving hugs around me. This connection felt safe and was filled with loving energy, reassurance, and a deep, heartfelt love that was different from my earthly loving connections. Grandma Catherine died when I was in my first year of college. I get reminders that she is with me when I see a streetlight go dark just ahead of me, and then turn back on as I drive under it. This makes me smile, and I know instantly that she is shining her love and light on me during this time. Sometimes, I hear jingling that reminds me of the sound car keys make when you rattle them. My grandmother did not drive, and she depended on others to take her to appointments or run errands. She would never ask to be taken anywhere unless it was essential, not wanting to be a bother to anyone. I loved taking her to buy a few groceries or run errands. Grandma never wanted me to wait long for her, so she was well prepared, with house keys in hand as we pulled into her driveway—thus my memory of jingling keys.

I often talk to her when driving, seeking advice or answers. I feel her presence, especially when I need a hug, or if I need some extra help handling life situations or making decisions. She seems to show up without me specifically asking her to be there, and she comes with immense feelings of love that leave tears in my eyes. I know when she is there because I feel enveloped in the warmth of her love. Early on, my connections with relatives that had crossed over were very private, and I did not tell others those experiences, not even close family members. Whenever I had the opportunity for a reading with someone that could connect with the dead, I would ask for my grandma to come forward. True to form, she was available to talk, usually even before I made the request. I realize now that during those readings, I really was looking for my own validation that I could indeed talk with her, and could feel her energy and the warmth of her love. I was looking for validation that the energy I was feeling was her—and that my experiences were truly happening at present in my life, and were not just a memory. Yes, it is real.

Long before I made a conscious effort to open myself to these connections for other people, at times the messages were so powerful that I would have no choice but to listen. I could easily feel hugs or bask in their love, but listening to and understanding their messages was different. Listening was actually the easy part. The difficult part was giving that message to the person it was intended for, and not knowing his/her beliefs about speaking with the dead. Would he be receptive to any messages? A part of me was still petrified that I would get the message wrong or misinterpret its meaning. I felt weighted down, and did not want to carry the enormous responsibility of delivering these messages.

So, for years I said nothing to anyone about this gift, and focused on connections with angelic beings, light beings, and my guides. I understand very clearly now that it is not my place to withhold this gift.

It is intended to be used to assist people in making those connections, and helping people hear the messages from their loved ones.

## Reaching Out to Kathy's Husband

When my children were young, I lost my best friend to cancer. Kathy and I had been friends since we were very little. She was a year older than me, and her brother was my age. My mom sometimes babysat her and her brother. We had a history together. We were awkward pre-teenagers in hideous lime-green polyester cheerleader attire, cheering for the Jets. We were on the speech team, and even when our high school activities split—mine toward cheerleading and sports, and hers toward speech, plays, and music—we continued to be friends. We worked together on weekends, and once decided, simply from sheer adventure and bravery, to switch cars for a week, mine being an automatic and hers a five-speed. This was when I refined my "expertise" in driving a manual transmission vehicle. Without her push, I probably never would have learned. We held deep trust for each other, and our friendship was one that remained solid even when we would not see each other for months. When we did, it was like we'd spoken just yesterday. She was maid of honor in my wedding, and was present at my son's birth. He knew her as Auntie Kathy with the tow truck, because she kept toys at her house for kids to play with when they were visiting. She never had any children in this lifetime, but many affectionately called her auntie, and she adopted all that would allow her to be an honorary auntie.

Kathy was happily married and busy with her career. Life got busy for both of us, and we did not see each other as much, but her death still hit me hard. She was this amazing, vibrant woman, and I was mad and sad that she was gone. Perhaps nine months to a year after her death, I began to feel her presence, and then I started to hear her messages. If I ignored them, they increased in intensity. Knowing her personality, she was not going to give up, especially if it was something urgent. She desperately wanted to reach out to her husband and was asking me for help. I could not possibly say no to my childhood friend.

First I had to phone Kathy's mother and ask for Doug's contact information. I was worried her mother would ask why I needed this, and more worried about the words I would choose to try to explain. I was never asked why, but once I had his number, it took me two days to work up the courage to make the call. I would sit and stare at the phone, and would hear my friend urge me to just dial the number. When I finally picked up the phone and dialed, I was nervous, and I am sure that my voice shook when I spoke. My mouth was dry, and no amount of water seemed to help resolve the feeling that I had sand in it.

I lied. Rather than tell Doug that I was speaking with Kathy, I told him that I had recently seen a psychic, and Kathy had come through with a number of messages specifically for him. I was not sure he believed in psychics, and asked if it was OK to tell him this information. He said yes, so I proceeded, not knowing exactly what was going to come out of my mouth, but trusting that with my dear friend's guidance all would be perfect. And it was.

The words began to flow. As I listened intently, Kathy's words floated within my mind. She kept saying *star-star-star*, and *name in lights*, *look at the stars*, *buy a star*. Cryptic words, but I knew the message was definitely something about buying a star. I asked Doug if any of this meant something to him. He said that he had never bought a star with her name on it, but Kathy's sister had approached him about planning an event where he could buy a star with her name on it as a way to honor her, and as a way to raise money for cancer research. This event was still in the planning process, and nothing had been formally settled yet. I said, "Doug, be prepared to buy a star, because Kathy was excited about this, and was counting on having her name in lights." I relaxed now, knowing the connection between them had just been established—and I would not need to interpret anything. It was simply my role to deliver the message, and the recipient would understand. My friend was teaching me how this process was to work. Again I felt her love wrap around me, and I let her words flow through me.

Kathy next talked about food, and then something about him not cooking or knowing how to cook. She wanted him to cook, or learn to. The words were fuzzy but urgent. As I repeated them, he stopped me and said that he actually was a very good cook, but had not felt like eating. An already thin man, he had lost twenty pounds since she died. This was Kathy's way of telling him to please cook and eat. She was worried about how he was taking care of himself. The remainder of our phone conversation turned more to him asking questions about how she was doing, and her talking to him about moving forward. I could see her— smiling, healthy, and happy—and it was important that he know she was happy, healthy, and just as beautiful as prior to her fight with cancer. I felt honored to be the conduit for their conversation. This truly was their time to connect and heal. That night I slept very soundly. It was as if Kathy and Doug now had closure, and I had completed my very small piece of the overall puzzle.

A few days later I meditated, with the intent to connect again with my dear friend Kathy. Gone was any fear about making this connection. This time her messages were for me. She was happy that I had finally taken on my purpose after years of sidestepping my gift. She had been with me on this journey, and had seen me dabble and be curious, but then step back. She was extremely happy that I had stepped forward, and not sideways or backward. I could feel her happiness and her joy. Kathy was happy and carefree, with a feeling of freedom in her energy that she did not have in the last few years of her life. Her words to me: *You do not need to fight so hard for that which is already yours.* This made perfect sense. These words continue to resonate with me even today. If it is too much work, then it is just not meant to be. When life seems hard, and it feels like you are swimming against the natural flow of the universe's energy, it is time to stop and assess exactly what it is you are trying to do. This would be a lesson I would continue to use while working with clients. If the connection with a loved one that has passed is too difficult to make, then the timing is off—and a better time will come later.

All connections that are made change us in one way or another. Whether it is to bring closure or to answer our questions, or whether it is simply a realization that our loved ones are around us, we are changed in how we look at the loving connections in our lives.

## Grandpa Joe

Before I went public with my gifts, I would do private readings for close friends. One such time I did a reading with a dear childhood friend. I wanted to try something new and do a calendar reading for her. This is where I work with the angel cards, building a calendar with messages for each month and what areas to focus on. This was a practice I had rarely done except with those closest to me, myself, or my children.

Below is part of an e-mail she sent to her aunt after that reading, where her grandfather showed up for the first time.

> Then…Laurie really blew me away. I pulled the card for February, and the word was "power." She said that is acceptance of myself, my personal power. Then she stopped and struggled a bit and asked me if I have a Grandpa Joe. I said yes, but he is gone. She nodded, and said that he wants me to know that I am incredible, and he is forever here for me, he is always around me. Okay…I have never heard Laurie swear. She was trying to convey the message, and she stopped and said, "I have to say it just like he's telling me," and she said, "I worked damn hard my whole life, but I know what is important, and I am here for you." Damn hard. That word—damn. That's my grandpa. She said that he is all energy, and she gestured with her arms in the air. I was a puddle of tears by now. That's Gramp, my Italian Gramp, who swore like a champ, and was in constant motion. Laurie never met my Gramp. She certainly would not know or remember his name—if she ever knew it in the first place. She certainly did not know that he died two years ago. She did not know he was Italian, so she could not have stereotyped. All I could do is cry. How could she know this?

I know Grandpa Joe has shown up for her many times since that initial reading. His message to her at that time was an opening to reassure her about her life journey, to send her love, and to let her know that she is supported by all those that love her deeply. She tells me that Grandpa Joe shows up for her, and even for her mother, his daughter. She tells me how nice it is to know and really feel that Gramp is with them. She hoped he had been with her since he died, and this affirmed that he remained very much a part of her life.

My friend tells me how one of my readings changed things. Again, it was not me changing her, but rather her own openness to acknowledge the connection. The connection had been there, because our connections to our loved ones don't simply stop. My reading with her became the affirmation of this connection, and that our loved ones are present.

## A Family of Three

The ability to communicate with our loved ones after they have passed is possible. They reach out to us, they send love, they talk to us, and they want to connect. One such memorable session was when I was doing readings for a family of three at my home. As I did individual readings for each in the privacy of my office, the others used my formal living room as a sitting area while waiting their turn. As I began my reading with the third family member, messages came through that she was highly intuitive but, out of fear, was not opening up her gifts to herself, or the world. The angelic beings wanted her to know that she was safe, and she was to begin to trust the things she felt, especially in highly charged areas.

In a second, my mother joined us. She passed a number of years ago, and will come to visit when I invite her in, but it is rare that she will join me during any of my readings with clients. Instantly, I understood her purpose for joining us. She had made her presence known to my client as a way of showing her it was safe to ask about her own gift of sensing the energies of those that had died. She was in a safe environment with someone that could answer her questions. The moment I acknowledged my mother in my own mind, my client asked me if my mother had passed. I said yes, and asked this client to describe my mom if she could, and to tell me what she was saying. As my client spoke my mother's words, I could hear her words being spoken directly to me as well—they were one and the same. This client needed validation that it was real, and she was in an environment to test her gift. She needed validation, much like I needed validation many years ago, and my purpose on that day was as a teacher.

## Validations

My own validation of information available to us, and how solid these connections are, came at a local event. I typically do not attend group-reading events, but on this day a panel of psychic readers would answer questions from the audience. I was being pushed to attend, and did not understand why I needed to be there, but trusted my own intuition to just go. As I sat in the audience, I thought perhaps there would be a burning question that I would be requested to ask. As I continued to wait, I felt a peaceful wave of energy move over me, and it was then that I understood my purpose was to simply observe. As each person stepped to the microphone and asked his/her question, I quickly wrote down the information I received before any answers were given from the panel. I listened to the responses; my answers mirrored the panelists' answers (or in some cases did not), yet all were accurate. My purpose on this day was purely for validation: I was ready to go public. No more hesitation that my gift was real; it should not be kept shadowed in my own life. I had important work to do. This also meant allowing these angelic connections to happen when they were intended to take place.

As I sat in that audience, I was overwhelmed by the gift I had just received in simply knowing it is real. I was given proof, the proof I was looking for, and then a deep knowing that it is *all* true. After thousands of connections, I have a greater understanding of the healing that is available to us when we are able to connect. I still have the occasional client that wants to test this—and me. I understand the world has skeptics, but I do not desire for people to spend their time with me "testing." The time is meant to be spent making the connection with their loved ones, for I truly get out of the way and become a conduit for the messages to come to them. In these thousands of readings, I have learned it is not my place to interpret the messages or put my words to them. If a terse word comes through, I will double-check if that is truly the word to be used; if it is, then I say it. A reading is meant to become a dialogue between the client and those to whom they wish to speak. When I get out of the way, and let the words flow through me, my clients get to hear the words or phrases of their loved ones, and that in itself helps the client understand that it is a true connection.

One such reading was with a client who had lost her mother. Her mother explained how it felt for her in words that were familiar to her daughter. The mother ended her description saying that her cancer had been *awful-awful-awful*, such an awful time, and she was so glad to be done with it. The daughter began to laugh, and told me that was exactly how her mother would have looked at it, and it was indicative of how she looked at other life events. No sugarcoating, stating the fact, but able to quickly move through the event. For this mother-daughter connection, the daughter needed to hear that it was indeed her mother coming through; that she made the transformation and was now at peace. This was her validation.

I love reading e-mails from my clients or hearing stories that start with, "Do you remember when you told me _____? It happened/came true." Recently I did a reading for Madeline. She was so excited to see me again, and in setting up an appointment, she made it very clear she wanted one as soon as possible. When I met with her, the first thing she said was that her daughter had gotten the job. Not *a* job, but *the* job. The details of her past reading were unclear, so I asked her to please remind me. The messages that had come through for her were that her daughter would have three interviews, and the third interview would result in a job offer, but it would not be in the field she was expecting. She would be very happy, and in the end, she would do very well. Her daughter did indeed have three interviews, and the third was for a position she had at first thought of not even applying for, but then decided she would at least go to the interview, if only for the practice. She was offered the job after this interview, in a new field, and she loved her new position.

I typically do not retain what is said at a reading for a number of reasons. Firstly, I do readings for so many people that I cannot possibly keep track of everyone's messages, family members, and life events. Secondly, these messages or events are for the client and his/her loved ones—I am only a bystander. Intimacy and privacy are involved in all our lives, and the angels keep it clean for boundary's sake. Lastly, messages and information may change depending on where an individual is in his/her life, and what decisions or actions have been chosen. We have free will, and this means that we have influence in the outcome. For example, an intuitive may tell you that she sees you taking a new job, but if you choose not to look for a job or not to take a new job, you are providing the path on your journey, and you have control over those outcomes. With Madeline's daughter's interviewing, if she had chosen not to go on that last interview, she would not have landed that job.

Sometimes a message or an experience will linger with me, or I will feel the experience so deeply that it stays with me for a long time. This happens when the love between the one that has died and the client is so deep that it brings tears to my eyes.

Such was a recent case where a mother was connecting with her daughter who had died. The love the daughter had for her mother was so great that I could not help but cry. I thanked the daughter for sharing this feeling, which left me deeply grateful for being able to experience that love. It is the energy work that I do on this earth that allows me to take this sort of love, and then envelop the client with energy. I often see loved ones hugging clients. Sometimes it is a full-on bear hug, or it might be a shoulder squeeze. Sometimes it is a kiss to the forehead. These actions are similar to or the same as what the loved one would have taken when on earth, and remain unique to the client and the loved one.

# Chapter 2

# How They Speak to Us

Our loved ones sometimes work very hard to send us messages in ways that only we would understand. Frequently I am asked if our loved ones send us signs—and the answer is yes. Many times we do not recognize these signs, or we reason them away as being just coincidence or something else. This is often when our analytical brains attempt to apply logic to something that may feel illogical.

## Husband Makes Himself Known

One such client, whose husband had died a number of years ago, called me. She felt sure that her husband was trying to communicate to her, and wanted to know if indeed he was. I asked her to tell me what she was experiencing, and before she even said her first two words, I felt her husband's energy, and I could smell freshly ground coffee. I am not a coffee drinker, and don't have coffee in my home, but the distinct smell of coffee was undeniable. He wanted to make the connection with her, but she was not hearing him. I could sense how hard he was trying to reach her. She continued, saying how she missed him dearly, and told me a memory. While he was alive, she would get so mad at him when he would spill coffee grounds all over the counter. She was forever scolding him to close the silverware drawer because he would spill coffee grounds everywhere, including in that drawer, which was directly in front of the coffeemaker. She was feeling sad that she had scolded him so much because she understood that he often could not stop his body from shaking, and he did not spill the coffee grounds to irritate her. She repeated that he was trying to reach her. Then I heard his words, telling me that *she* had spilled coffee grounds in the drawer that morning.

When I said this, first there was silence on the phone, and then she started laughing. Yes, it was true, and was something that she *never* had done before. It was almost as if someone had knocked her hand, purposely making her spill. Then she asked: had her husband joined her in the kitchen that morning, and had he intentionally knocked her hand to the point she had spilled those coffee grounds? She was happy to hear that it was his energy that had indeed joined her. She also wanted him to know that she got his message loud and clear, and if he wanted to continue to knock those coffee grounds out of her hand, she would be OK with that. Yes, he was sending a message to her that she would understand.

## Things That Go Bam in the Night

Years ago, when my children were small, we lived in another home. I was in a deep, deep sleep in the middle of the night, and was woken up by the sound of an explosive-like boom. It was one of those startling events that shake you, but when in such a deep sleep, you wonder if it was something you dreamed, or if it actually happened. The fear I felt at that moment kept me in my bed, wondering if it was safe to move. Eventually, I got out of bed and looked around the entire house. I could not feel or see anything that appeared out of place, but I still felt uneasy. I could not sleep the rest of the night. The next day that uneasiness stuck with me, and I kept hearing my grandmother's voice saying to check the furnace. I did, and outwardly, it appeared fine. It was providing heat, and nothing looked odd. It was the middle of a very cold winter, and I reasoned it away as a bad dream, perhaps brought on by fears that it would stop running while I was scheduled to be out of town. I did not want my family to have to deal with no heat. I was uneasy about leaving town, and arranged for the furnace be fully checked by a professional. I was in England when I got a phone call: the furnace had been checked, and a huge crack was found that was emitting dangerous carbon monoxide into the house. The furnace service company would not even let it be run, and had shut it down until a new one could be installed. I asked if the loud boom I had heard could have been the crack, and the repairman said no, but I had been very lucky that I had insisted on a professional looking at it.

I hung up the phone in disbelief. I took a moment to go to the restroom to compose myself, and to talk to my grandma. I had a deep appreciation for her diligence in talking to me, and her persistence in the messages that it was the furnace, and that I needed to have a professional help. She had warned me, and by doing so—and by my listening—I was able to prevent something that had the potential to be disastrous for our family.

I tell people that when they get a feeling, which can be an uneasy one, they should pay attention to it. They should not so easily reason it away as just a feeling. These feelings we get that seem odd to us, or come from seemingly nowhere, can be a message we need to pay attention to. There have been numerous stories of people that have had an urge to change traffic lanes on a busy road, only to have a near miss, and a realization that if they had stayed in that previous lane they would have gotten into an accident.

Some clients may be shy about asking if what they've experienced actually happened. They may begin their sentence with, "This may sound crazy, but…" I reassure them that in all the connections I have made, there have been none that I would call crazy—maybe different, but never crazy.

## The Pixie Knows

At times I do workshops or parties where I speak to a larger group. On one occasion, I was asked to speak at a local women's circle. The circle was held in the facilitator's studio connected to her home. When I began to speak, a little pixie that lives in the house startled me. I made multiple attempts to ignore this distraction, but after watching this energy float insistently past my face multiple times, I realized I could not avoid sharing what I was experiencing. The look on my face was either amusement or curiosity, for this was like a child that was not going to give up until I acknowledged him. The women around the circle probably thought it was whimsical, or even odd, when I paused and turned to the studio owner to ask her if she knew she had a pixie running around the room. She felt this was very significant, as she had been seeing this pixie for years. He would show up in her peripheral vision, but was never directly visible. He would often dodge from one room to another so she could barely see him. She thought it had perhaps become a game for him to see if she would notice him. She fondly referred to him and his mates as Little People, as she thought there were more, and he reminded her of the leprechauns of Ireland or the Little People of Native American lore. In one of his many dashings past my face, I asked if he would stop and tell me his name. He didn't stop, but as he moved away, I distinctly heard him announce himself as Sammy or Samuel. He was an energy that maybe did not like all our energy in this room, but was quite satisfied that I had seen him. As quickly as he had joined us, he was gone.

A month or two following that event, the studio owner's home was broken into. She contacted me and asked if perhaps I could check in with Sammy to see if he had seen anything that day. Possibly he could help with what happened, and provide some information or a description of who broke in. I sat quietly and asked if Sammy could please connect with me. I could sense his energy, and a bit of fear in that energy. I knew he liked that home and its owners, and although he was shy, he wanted to help them.

Sammy told me that there were two young males, around eighteen to twenty years old. I passed this information on to the home owner. I asked Sammy if he could indicate what type of car they had driven. I immediately saw what I believed was a dark green or dark blue SUV, maybe a Suzuki. Later, the home owner heard that a potential victim in the same neighborhood had spotted two young men, and reported them driving a vehicle that was a dark blue Suzuki. Sammy told me that at first he thought the two young males were at the home to play, and he was excited, but when he realized they were up to no good, he hid.

The home owner asked me if I thought they would get any of their belongings back. I felt they would get a few pieces of jewelry (which they did), and perhaps get a few other items back at a much later time. I felt the need to reassure Sammy that the home owners were not angry, nor would anyone hurt him, but it seemed more important that he know his home owners were safe. In this case, the little pixie, Sammy, provided valuable information about the incident, but this also was a case where the home owners believed this little pixie might know something that would help them solve the crime or feel better about their belongings.

The two young men were caught shortly after the incident and were sentenced appropriately. Actually the SUV was black, and another make that the police said was often mistaken for a Suzuki. The home owner continues to see glimpses of the pixie energy, and she likes knowing he and his mates continue to frolic in and around the gardens of the home, keeping watch now.

# When There Are No Words

Every client is told that I am simply a participant in making many connections happen. This is really his/her time to make the connection, and to ask questions. No questions are silly or dumb, and probably few questions would surprise me. I keep paper in my office for those that would like to write anything down—and a box of tissues for the tears that may be shed when a connection is felt. I am blessed to be in the proximity of some of the most profound reconnections. Sometimes there are no words, and sometimes those tissues have been for me. Such times are the meetings where I find myself unable to put into words the overwhelming waves of love that I feel being bestowed on the client. These times make me weep from the deepness of this love. I am only a bystander in this love, yet I cannot help but be in the middle of it because the love is so immense. I am able to sense or see a loved one reaching out energetically and touching or hugging his/her loved one. Sometimes the loved one can feel the hug, or feel the warmth of a gentle touch to his arm or back. Sometimes it is a light touch that creates goose bumps on her skin. I remind that person not to ignore these feelings, because these are very real energetic hugs, touches, and pulses of love that she is feeling. My clients are feeling them for a reason, and more than likely, it is a loved one that is reaching out to get their attention. There may not be words, or sounds, but there is feeling, and usually with this feeling is emotion, and sometimes with this emotion, tears.

I remind my clients it is a healthy release, and if they are focused more on fighting the tears or their emotions, they are less focused on what they are feeling or hearing as they make that connection. I often ask them to relax and just "be" with the emotion. Most often, if they are able to relax, they quickly become enveloped in the feeling of loving warmth. This is what their loved ones want them to feel—all the love they are pouring over them.

It is very important to spend time within yourself so you are familiar with your own feelings and emotions. This makes it easier to recognize feelings that are not yours. This clarity in turn allows you to feel external energies that influence your energies.

A mother whose son had died arranged to meet with me. As she entered my office, I could sense her son following. She settled into the chair, and I could see her struggle, attempting to hold back tears. When she asked if her son was still with her, I said he was there now. She gave a huge sigh of relief, but then wondered why she could no longer feel his presence. She said that soon after he had died she could feel his presence very close to her, and she worried that he had gone away since it was more difficult to feel him now. He stood very close to her, and was reaching out, so I could see his energy overlap hers. She was so focused on trying to remember and feel his earthly physical presence, along with trying to hold in the tears, that she was not allowing herself to feel the energy-charged sense of his loving presence. We sat for some time in silence, working on identifying how this energy feels, and letting go of all beliefs of how it should feel, but rather sense how it *is* feeling. It took a while to reconnect at that level, but she was able to let go and allow her senses to open up, and just be in the energy. Without any words, she could feel his love all around her.

## My Guides Keep Me on Track

I work very closely with the Archangel Michael, the Archangel Metatron, and my shaman. My shaman first called to me while I was in Sedona, Arizona. Over time, he has been a guide to assist me on my journey by keeping me on track. Most noticeably, I would know that I was off track when he put his face up to mine. I guess he was worried I would not pay attention to him unless he did something so bold, and something I couldn't ignore. I am grateful for the presence of his energy. I often see him dance with joy as I realize that I am exactly where I need to be. When I am off track too far, I will begin to feel his energy before the in-the-face maneuver. Most recently, light beings have joined us to provide additional education or responses that feel more analytical in nature versus the from-the-heart messages with which I have become so familiar. For those that are close to me here in Minnesota, you understand how I dislike the cold weather. I can be seen wearing not-so-stylish layers because at some point it is all about the warmth, and not so much energy is spent on how it looks. When I work with angels and guides, sometimes the energy in the room elevates to the point where the windows must be opened—even in the middle of winter—because I am unable to cool off. I tell clients that if they suddenly feel warm or begin to sweat, they should know the angelic beings have arrived and are ready to work.

When my grandmother comes to me, I feel her energy in my heart. It makes me smile, and I can feel the energy move through my entire body. I call this a hug, and I thank her for allowing me to feel this and know it is her. I feel her most while I am alone in the car. Perhaps it is the combination of the memory of driving with her along, and with being open to her presence. No words; only the feeling of warmth and joy.

# When Words Mean Everything

One summer day, a client brought her father to see me. He was in Minneapolis visiting his family after his wife had crossed over that spring. His daughter had scheduled a reading for him before he was to travel back to his home state, so I met with them early on a Sunday morning. When they arrived, I asked the father to step into my office first, and his daughter stayed in our home's formal living area. I do not know exactly how long I spent with him, but the time was filled with messages from his wife and other loved ones. Angels there to assist in answering his questions and helping in any way they could surrounded him.

I recall very little of what was said, but will never forget the deep feeling of love that this wife had for her husband, and the physical warmth this love brought to my office. I could feel the intensity of the energy to the point that it made me weep. My office got so hot that I needed to turn on the ceiling fan. I tried as best I could to put this feeling into words for him, as her love continued to shower down over him. Then I was shown a boat. I needed to ask this man if he liked boating, had a boat, or if there was significance in this boat his wife was showing me. Yes, he loved boating, but his wife had hated it. She was telling him to remember his love of boating, and now it was time to enjoy it. He started laughing. He had been wondering the entire drive over to my house about what she would say, and what would be her messages. He had been worried about her crossing, and by acknowledging his presence, she had reassured him that she was all right, and it was OK that not all the family members could be present. He understood, and was at peace.

As he stood to leave, I handed him a sunstone shaped like a heart, and told him I usually give rose quartz hearts, but she wanted him to have this yellow stone for his pocket. Only she and he would understand the meaning in that. He smiled, gave me a hug, and put the stone in his pocket. I commended him for his openness in coming that day, but then I noticed the difference in his eyes. He had found a place of peace. Many of his questions had been answered, and more importantly, he knew that his wife was OK.

As part of my business, I offer parties where the host invites six to ten guests. I spend time with each person individually, and if there are any messages for the group I share those also. Recently at an intuitive party, the hostess's husband wanted to have his intuitive reading first. He met me at the door, introduced himself, and jokingly said, "Oh, but you are psychic so you already know that." I am very accustomed to being tested. I think some people have not used their gift with a pure heart, and have created some mistrust. In my early years of doing readings, I worried about being tested by clients, but I have long ago let that go. People continue to test, doubt, or not trust, and it may take a bit to help them relax to where they feel comfortable and trusting.

## Sue—When the Time Was Right

Sue scheduled time with me. She canceled and then rescheduled, then canceled and rescheduled again. Her fears were preventing her from coming to see me; however, I also knew that she had loved ones on the other side that were persistent in getting her to my front door. Eventually, she would be pushed beyond her fears. I felt this was going to be an important connection, but divine timing had a hand in making this appointment happen. Each time she called to cancel, I could hear the trembling in her voice, and she was overly apologetic. With each cancellation I would explain that when the timing was right, she would feel it. On the fourth attempt she kept her appointment, and she brought a friend with her. She asked if her friend could remain in the room, and I told her absolutely, as her friend could take notes and help her recount all the information she would be hearing.

I gave her a hug, and told her that her mother had requested the hug because she could not be physically present at her wedding. Her mother wanted her to know that she was at the wedding, and was very appreciative of the special prayer they said for her that day. Sue was speechless as tears rolled down her face. I continued to talk as Sue listened and her friend took notes. Sue's mother paused, and I knew she was waiting for a response. Sue turned to her friend and said that this message was exactly what they had been talking about during the car ride to my office. Sue wanted a message from her mother that only she would know. She wanted this validation that her mom had indeed been at her wedding, and had been with the family that day. Sue said she felt her mom's presence that entire day, but was seeking validation. The words of validation were about the special prayer that was said for her mother, written specifically for that day.

### The Apron Was the Clue

Early in my doing readings publicly, I did an intuitive party for a family. I did not know the full relationship of each of them until after I had done all their readings. When the first person settled in for her reading, I immediately saw her mother standing in a kitchen. She had an apron on, and was stirring something in a big bowl. She was not saying anything, but continued to turn toward and then away from me, the entire time stirring. She stood with her back to me. In my mind, I asked her if she had a message for her daughter. I did not get a response, but felt that the position of her in the kitchen was meaningful. There was definitely a reason why she continued to be in the kitchen, and this was the only thing I was sensing from her. I told the woman that her mother was not moving from the kitchen, and asked if there might be significance in her showing me this. Perhaps her mother loved to cook, or they spent very special moments talking or together as a family in the kitchen. As I was asking these questions, I continued to ask the mother if she had any words she would like to pass on. The mother continued to stir her bowl. The daughter looked at me and said, "Well, she died in the kitchen. Perhaps that is why she is showing you the kitchen." It was then that the mother stopped stirring, and gave her full attention to me and to her daughter. Before she would say anything, her mother needed validation that I could see her, and that her daughter would understand that it truly was her.

# Messages in Animals

We often get messages in a symbolic way from animals because of the significance in their presence. I am often asked if these are relatives presenting themselves, or are loved ones sending symbolism in the form of an animal. When I work with a group or am asked to host an intuitive party, I will take time prior to doing all the individual readings to share messages or information that my shaman or the angels want given. They often remind the group to pay attention and to be alert for signals and symbolism, especially messages through animals.

Almost a year ago I had done an intuitive party for this particular group of women. Helen had been getting inquiries about hosting another such event. She invited some friends that were not able to make it to her last party, as well as many of the women that had been at her first party and had asked if they could have another reading. These women were very knowledgeable about universal energies. They understood the energetic connections in all lifetimes, and many had made connections with their angels or loved ones when we were together last time. This was one of those events where I was approached and asked if I remembered when I said _____, and then it came true. I remind people that unless there is purpose for me to remember, I don't. Sometimes, if I am reminded of the message or information, I may recall pieces. Some readings are especially impactful, and I remember the connection very well.

## A Soaring Eagle

As Mary sat down across from me, she seemed vaguely familiar. She told me the last time we had met was right before her father passed away. Abruptly, her mother was in the room with us, reminding me of the rose quartz she had asked me to give to her daughter and her husband. She had politely asked if I could give two; one rose quartz for Mary, and one for Mary's father. She wanted Mary to give this heart to her father as a symbol that everything would be OK, and that she would be waiting for him on the other side when he passed. He died with the rose quartz stone heart in his hand.

Then, Mary said that near her father's passing, he spoke of seeing a great eagle soaring above him. He asked his daughter if she too saw this eagle. Mary described her father pointing up to the ceiling of the bedroom where he was seeing the eagle. Days after his death, Mary began to see eagles. She saw them when she was driving; she would see them when she went for a walk. She felt like everywhere she turned, she would see an eagle. She never saw eagles anywhere like this before, and she did not know if it was the same eagle or different ones, but she felt like they were everywhere. Around the same time, she visited the home of an elderly couple for a potential job opportunity to provide them home care. When they opened the front door, an eagle swooped down and, for a moment, everyone thought it would fly right in to the house. As they stood in awe, in her mind she asked if this was a symbol from her father, and if he was near. After she met with the elderly couple, she knew it was more than a symbol. This was definitely him being near her, but it was also him directing her to her next client, and down the path of finding purpose and direction in her life, and a longer-term career in providing service for homebound people, or people that needed some extra help around the house. Her father was very much involved in helping her and showing her what she needed to be doing now that he was gone. Even in the afterlife her father was reaching out to her, and there was a sense of comfort that all in her life would be fine.

Birds are very symbolic for many people. My aunt Doris loved cardinals, and was able to whistle exactly like them. As a young child, I was fascinated by her ability to seemingly attract and speak to cardinals. I was enamored by the bird feeders and birdbaths that speckled her yard. A few times I would stop there with my dad, and while he was busy in the garage with my uncle, I would follow my aunt around her backyard, filling the birdbaths and bird feeders. One year, she had a family of cardinals nesting in a hanging basket right outside the porch door, and every time I would go in and out, the mother bird would leave the nest, but when my aunt was around, she would remain in the basket, and the father bird would perch in a tree nearby. My aunt died when I was in my late thirties, but I held these memories of her and her connection to the cardinals. Standing at her grave the day she was buried, I could hear the distinct whistle of a cardinal off in the distance. As the priest continued his prayers, I looked around the cemetery, trying to spot where this cardinal was hiding. Other family members that knew this aunt well also began to look around. There was no hiding; in a lone bush thirty feet from where we stood was a brilliant red cardinal, singing its heart out to us. I do believe it was my aunt sending this wonderful bird to us, to remind us that our loved ones are never very far away. We just have to be alert, watch for the signs, and listen to any messages. As I watched this cardinal, I sent love to the heavens in acknowledgment that we had heard—and would think of her.

I am often asked to speak with groups such as book clubs, writers groups, quilting clubs, executive groups, yoga classes, or other business groups that may have an interest in what I do. On this occasion I was speaking to a yoga group, specifically about our personal energy and the vibrational frequency we emit, and how that assists us in connecting with those that have died. At the end of my talk, I asked if there were any questions. One woman asked if her husband was present. He was, and he showed me an airplane. I asked if he had been a pilot or loved to fly his own plane. She said yes. I was immediately shown a number of birds lying at my feet. Behind the woman, on the wall, was a trophy goose, but the birds at my feet were not geese. I thought perhaps that I was visualizing these birds as a connection with the goose somehow, so I asked to be shown again, and asked what I was supposed to know about these birds. I was then shown that they were pheasants, and were from a hunting trip, as now a dog was sitting proudly beside them. Yes, her husband was an avid hunter, and he wanted his wife to know that he was still hunting and enjoying the sport. These birds were very symbolic for her in knowing that her husband was still connected.

In my early twenties, I moved into my first home. As a welcoming gift, a friend thought I should have one of the kittens from her cat's litter. I had been more of a dog person, but I graciously accepted this cat. I named the kitten Boots, for his three white paws, and the fact that it was winter and he was forever climbing into my boots left by the door. I truly believe that in this cat's previous life he was a dog because each morning I would play fetch with him. As I was getting ready for work in the bathroom at the top of the stairs, I would throw a crumpled piece of paper down the stairs. Boots would retrieve it and drop it at my feet. This would go on until I would walk out the back door to drive to work. At night, I would feel Boots crawl under the blankets at the bottom of the bed and sleep against my feet. This cat was so protective of me that anyone entering my home would be attacked. One day, I came home from work and found the screen pulled out from the front window. Boots was sitting on the windowsill, and to this day, I believe that he prevented someone from breaking into my home. When I had the house for sale, I had to kennel overprotective Boots because he would not let anyone enter the house.

Friends would ask if I owned a cat or part guard dog. When I vacationed, they honestly told me they were petrified to enter my house alone. Boots moved with me when I sold that house, and shortly after got sick and needed to be put down. I was so upset with having to take this step that I asked another family member to please make that final trip to the veterinarian. I then felt overwhelmed with guilt that I had not been with him during his final minutes. Those first few nights I hardly slept. Then one night, as I was getting ready for bed, I felt Boots's presence. Sure enough, when I settled into bed, I could feel the blankets move, and a sinking feeling by my feet. I knew that Boots had found his way back to my bed. I needed him to know I missed him, and that I should have been with him during his last moments. I needed to know that he still loved me, and I did not abandon him. I felt his love, and this helped me heal from losing a pet that was very special. I did not feel his presence each night, but every once in a while I would feel him crawl into bed and rest against my feet, and each time I would acknowledge him and the safety that he brought with him.

Since that time, I have had several pets that have crossed over, and they all have at one point or another come to visit. I believe this is to let me know that they are OK. I continue to send them love as they continue their journey beyond.

# Messages in Music

We also receive information or messages from our loved ones, the angels, or our guides through sound or music. I did private readings for two sisters whose mother had died of cancer the previous summer. She had been very specific about requesting that one song be played at the ceremony, while all other details of the funeral were left to the family. It was a song that her daughters had never heard before, but they honored her wish and assured her that it would be played at the ceremony. Since the mother's passing, they heard that song on the radio numerous times during the day. Both were astounded that neither had heard the song before, yet after their mother's funeral, they heard it daily. One daughter said that she could not get in her car each day without hearing that song. She said it was a very nice song, but hearing it was almost driving her crazy. She acknowledged that she believed it was her mother reminding her that she was still there, and it was her way of sending a very special message. As we talked, she acknowledged that it was a particularly hard time in her life with other things happening, and she was missing having her mom around. She wanted advice from her mom, and even though she knew her mom was present, she did not know how to hear her mother's words of advice. I suggested that the next time she heard that song, she should pay attention to the very next song or the following advertisement she heard on the radio.

A few months later I did get a follow-up e-mail from one of the sisters. She reminded me of her reading, and said that the advice to listen to the radio for the next song or commercial after the "offending" song was the best advice she'd been given. She said that her mom was giving her all sorts of advice in the words of a commercial advertising a special on new cars. She needed a new car and didn't know if now was the time. She also was not sure if she should remain at her job. One day as she was contemplating this, she heard the song "Should I Stay or Should I Go" by the Clash. Her mom had sung this to her one time when she was younger and couldn't make up her mind. This was her mom's method of communicating to her that she was right there in the car, helping her assess what she could do. Stay or go.

When I speak at events, groups, or do private readings, I often remind people to pay attention to symbols, signs, and the messages that are being sent. The world is full of messages and insight. We just have to be alert and aware.

My mother's father played the mandolin. He would carry it in his car, and many times we would beg him to bring it into the house and play for us. I was fascinated watching his hands move over the neck of the instrument while his fingers plucked out some of our favorite tunes. "Edelweiss" was a show tune made famous in the 1959 Rodgers and Hammerstein musical *The Sound of Music*, and it was my favorite song. Years later on a business trip to Germany, I found a music box in a shop near our hotel that played "Edelweiss." I shrieked with such joy that co-workers traveling with me continued to tease me for many months.

When my mother was dying from cancer and was at a hospice facility, we would take turns sitting with her. She was not able to respond, but we all felt it important to be with her and let her know we loved her. My older brother would bring his guitar and sing for her. Sometimes he would sit in the main sitting room and play for anyone that could join him. He would play some of his favorites, but he would also ask if people had requests. I was sitting with my mom, and could hear him playing the very distinctive "Edelweiss." I left her room and entered the main room to see that he had not even been playing. The guitar sat in its case. I stopped in mid-step, turned, and returned to my mother's room. As I sat back down, I heard the music again. This time, I knew that when it was her time to go, her father was reaching out and would meet her with loving arms. I asked her if she could hear his music, and said that was to let her know it was going to be fine. She crossed over on his birthday.

Sometimes, I catch a certain phrase I have not heard before in a particular song. After hearing the song over and over again, for whatever reason, a particular phrase sticks out. It is almost as if I am hearing it for the first time. I find that this happens when I am in search of messages or an answer for something that is happening in my life. I ask my angels, guides, or my loved ones to please send me information. I also ask that they make it easy for me to understand or grasp. Then, I pay attention. If this happens with a phrase in a song, it is usually information to assist me. Music places us in a higher vibration, where we are more able to connect with the higher energies such as angels, guides, light beings, and our loved ones—and it makes us feel better.

When I was growing up, my mother had music playing as she worked in the kitchen or cleaned the house. I have loved music, but I find that as I get older, it is more important to have sound around me. It is usually music, as the television is rarely on in our house.

## Creaks and Moans

Clients ask about noises in their homes, such as creaks and groans they think their house is making, but really are wondering if it is something else. I tell them that our loved ones never want us to be afraid. If the creaks or groans of the floorboards scare them, this would not be a loved one, and is probably movement of the house. Especially here in Minnesota during the winter months, our houses seem to adjust more with the dryness of the weather. We have floorboards that creak in our present house. One night, I happened to be awake when I heard them. As I peered into the hallway, I was met by the stare of our big orange tabby—a kitty going for a midnight run around the house, very much alive. When our loved ones come to us, they come with love, and generally we will feel the warmth of this love.

# Messages in Dreams

Sometimes we may get information or messages in our dreams. Numerous clients have told stories of being asleep and feeling their loved one sitting on their bed. One such client was struggling with the sale of her childhood home. She felt that she should remain in the house after her parents died so that it would stay in the family. She believed this was what her father would want. She was hesitant to admit that she was struggling with the demands of the home, and deep down she desired to sell it and buy something smaller. To help her with this decision, I asked for her parents to come forward so they could help answer her questions about what to do with the house. Feeling her father's presence, I asked him what he would like his daughter to do. I could see him extend his arms outward from his sides in a motion, as if he were sweeping the room, and then he would drop his arms to his sides. I told the client, and asked if this meant anything to her. She stared wide-eyed at me, then proceeded to explain that she'd had a dream where her father was standing in her bedroom, and he kept making these sweeping arm movements. In that dream, he told her to sell the house, but she thought the dream was only her wish to do so, and not a message from him. She realized at that moment that he was indeed telling her it was OK to sell. These motions or information meant nothing to me, but fit with her dream, and she fully understood what he was saying.

The angels have told me, and have asked me to teach others, a method to communicate with them or ask for information. I follow this practice very often when I am feeling stuck in a situation or am at a place in my life that I feel I need some additional help or insight for what direction to take or decision to make. This can be done many ways, but the easiest method is to write down your questions before going to sleep, and ask that the answers come to you in your dreams—and that you understand these dream messages. You may not recall your dreams, but you may find that you do get insight into your question.

A number of years ago, I was planning a family vacation. We were all excited, and looked forward to this time together. We did this a couple of times a year, and this year was going to be no different, or so I thought. For almost a week, I would wake up with this deep feeling of dread, and I could feel it in the pit of my stomach. I was not able to pinpoint exactly what was causing this dread, but as a result of this feeling, I avoided making the necessary travel arrangements. In my head, I wanted to take this trip, but in my heart, I could not help but delay any planning, and the feeling of excitement was also diminished. Something was definitely off, and my feelings were pushing me to pay attention. Each night I would write out my question right before I went to sleep, and ask that the information be provided in my dreams or other messages. In doing so, I put myself on alert to be aware of thoughts, messages, ideas, or conversations that might provide insight.

My project at work was put on hold, so it provided the opportunity to take a break at that time, rather than waiting until our planned spring break time frame. Someone I worked with had a certificate for an amusement park at that vacation spot, and would not be able to use it before it expired, so offered it to me. I checked online for plane tickets, and found I could get a package vacation for less than half of what we had originally budgeted. This vacation fell together with such ease that it would have been hard *not to go*. We cancelled our original vacation and went on this newly planned vacation, and enjoyed our time immensely.

The feeling of dread did not go away; rather, it now turned into a feeling of needing to be home at the time we had originally planned our trip. That put me on a different alert, one that centered on my home and kids. It was that year that my son became extremely ill and spent a week in intensive care. Had we been on the originally planned vacation, we would have been out of state when he got sick, and the results would have been drastically different for him and all of us. Being home during that time provided family and friends for support and help, and he was with his normal medical team that knew him and could quickly provide what he needed. We all agreed that our angels where watching over us, including our vacation scheduling.

Other times the messages may be simple problem-solving ideas, or information on actions we are to take, and they can take on a more lighthearted feeling. Recently, my son and I were talking about the energy of the rocks in my house, and how I had a desire to make that energy more accessible and appealing for people. That night I went to sleep without asking any specific questions, but I had crazy dreams of rocks hanging from my dining room blinds. In my dreams, I had been shown very specifically what I needed to do, and how my son would be involved. The next morning I told my son, and when he asked where the completed work would be hung, I told him about the dream. What I had seen was he would hang the rocks from my dining room blinds. In this case, the messages were about creating these healing energy strings of rocks to be made available for people to simply hang in their homes. The intent of this creative work was clear to both of us. My son said he had not dreamed about this same project, but his knowing of exactly what he needed to do told me that this information was probably known to both of us, and perhaps he just did not recall dreaming.

## Questions for Your Subconscious

When you want information to come to you in your dreams and it is not clear, or you feel you received no response, do not give up. Write the same question each night until you get an answer. You also must be open to whatever the answer is, and then trust it. Years ago I had interviewed for a position that I really wanted. Believing in the power of positive thought, I continued to send out energy that I was actually in this position, yet I had a sense it was not going to happen. Each night I would write out my question on the paper I left next to my bed, asking that they please share the outcome. One morning, before I even opened my eyes, I saw in my mind's eye, and then I heard it: *you are not ready for this position*. I took this to mean that in a future time I would be better prepared, and I would have the opportunity then. No longer did I linger on this position, and stopped giving it any of my energy; instead, I focused on my current job and other aspects of my life. By doing this, it allowed me to quickly move through any disappointment, and just move forward. As I look back at that time in my life, I believe my guides were keeping me on track with my current job, which led to many opportunities that would not have been available if I had taken another job. And looking back at my skills, they were right; I was not ready. I truly believe if it is meant to be, then it will be, and if it is not meant to be, then it will not happen. This was one of those times.

A number of times people ask about déjà vu. At a recent private reading with an eleven-year-old girl and her mother, the young girl explained that she often feels she has experienced that exact moment, comment, or event before. She explained an entire event in her classroom where her friend dropped a book, then stumbled as she picked it up. The teacher was teasing her about why she dropped her book, and was reminding her to tie her shoes next time. As she was watching, then listening to her friend and the teacher have this interaction, she felt that she had already witnessed it—perhaps in an dream—and that's why it felt so familiar. This happens often, and she is uncomfortable because she does not know why it feels like she is reliving these moments. She does not remember her dreams, but assumed she forgot these dreams.

This may be the case, but it also may be her ability to play forward what is happening, and in doing so, it only feels like she is reliving it, when actually she is only living it at that moment. Many gifted people have moments where they receive information just prior to it happening; thus, when it happens they feel it is déjà vu.

Clients often talk about the dreams they have about their deceased loved ones, and wonder if this is their loved one reaching out to them. Yes, it is. How quickly we attempt to reason away that it is something our mind has made up, rather than viewing it as a gift from our loved ones that they have connected with us.

Recently I was telling two of my friends about the fun adventure I had with them in a dream. We were in a tropical location and were sliding down a waterfall. In the dream, I was the last one to slide down, as I was assessing how we would ever get back to the top. It would be impossible to climb the waterfall. For me, it was symbolism to just let go of my worries or those things in my life that I was trying so hard to control, and just have fun. Go with the flow, and in this case it was the flow of this enormous waterfall that went out to the ocean. My friend said that she had also been having very vivid dreams lately, and in the last one, she and her husband waited for a train in Rome, Italy, with Grandpa Joe. She interpreted this as him sending her a message that he was very much with her, and part of her life, including seeing her recent marriage, because they had discussed the possibility of traveling to Italy.

# Chapter 3

## Meeting with a Psychic

Prior to any readings, I ask the client to write out his/her questions sometime within twenty-four hours of the reading. If clients want to speak to anyone in particular, I ask them to write that person's name, and to ask that person to be present for them during the reading. Not every psychic does this, and it is not the only way to connect and receive information. I do this for a number of reasons. First, it is to get permission for the information to be available for me to hear and understand. Without this simple granting of permission, it would feel like I am invading a person's space or privacy. After seeing the look of fear on people's faces when they hear I am an intuitive reader, this became my common practice. They are fearful that I might know something about them they do not want anyone to know about, or that I might see or hear something bad is about to happen to them or their loved ones. I tell clients that I have this same practice with my children. They would not want me intruding in their privacy, and overall just knowing everything in their lives. I do not walk around the grocery stores and snoop into other people's lives. The angels would not allow that, and I honestly have enough busyness in my life without pulling in any other information. When I meet with a client, I focus solely on that person. If I am meeting with a group, I focus on the individual that is receiving the message. All other energies become blurry for me, and only the energy that I am focusing on remains clear.

The second reason I ask my clients to write out their questions is it provides them focus during the reading—on specific questions or areas of their life that they want to obtain information. Often the information comes so fast or they get distracted with what they are hearing that they may forget to ask all their questions. This also allows me to focus my energy on the client's particular questions and answers, and helps eliminate any possible side chatter.

At times, a client will hear messages beyond the information he sought. When this happens, I tell him that is information relevant to what is occurring in his life or urgent messages that need to be heard, or he may be thinking of asking the question, but is afraid or hesitant. A reading may go in a totally different direction, based on what clients are asking, and what they are open to hearing. They may ask anything, but generally the messages that come through are direct answers to their questions.

Lastly, I follow this practice because it is my communication with the energies from beyond that offers a time and a place for the messages to come through. I have done readings for clients who, even though they are curious and want to experience the reading, are afraid. Perhaps they have had a bad experience, or have heard of someone having a bad experience. It is quite normal to be hesitant, especially if you've never experienced a connection with a loved one that has crossed over. I acknowledge that it is all right that they feel nervous or afraid, and then I ask for the angels to come in and assist in helping the client to relax. I do this by asking that the energy be for the highest good of the client. This simply means that I am asking that the energies and messages be solely for the benefit of the client. Anything that would not be of benefit, or anything that is not of the highest, purest energy, would not be expressed.

Sometimes a client approaches the reading and simply asks who's with me, or what I should know. A few times I am not able to sense anyone with them, or I sense the loved one but he/she is saying nothing. If the energy says nothing, it is pausing as a means to allow the client to ask questions. This may also mean that the client may not truly want a reading, or the fear is so deep that no information can come through because whatever the message may be, the person may not believe anyway. In these cases, I ask for their guides or my guides to step in to help, or I can ask a close family member that has died to enter and provide some signals or signs that the client would understand.

The best preparation the clients can do is to think about the questions they want answers to, write them down, and think about the loved ones to whom they would like to connect. They also should ask themselves what fears they may have, and tell the intuitive/psychic. This allows the angels and guides to help where possible to remove these fears. If you are the person having the reading, you may also ask that all information be shared with you for your highest purpose or potential. This means you are only receptive to information, energy, or messages that are good for you.

Clients are also experiencing energy work while I am working with them. This means that I am centering their aura energy, and if they were feeling sluggish, or jittery from stress or anxiety, I am balancing this energy out to more peaceful levels. When I connect with the angels, guides, and light beings, the frequency of my energy field is elevated. This means that clients are also exposed to higher levels of vibrational energy during the reading. This leaves the client feeling at peace or in a euphoric state as his/her vibrational frequency is moved to a more balanced level or is slightly elevated. When we are joyful, happy, in love, or at peace with our lives, our energy levels are balanced and we are vibrating at a higher frequency. When we are tired, stressed, depressed, have anxiety, are worried, or are not nutritionally balanced or hydrated, our energy levels vibrate at a lower frequency, perpetuating our feeling of tiredness, a lack of passion for life, and downright feeling blah. When I am finished with my readings, clients should feel at peace, calm, and filled with love in their hearts.

# Chapter 4

# Unexpected Messages

At another intuitive party, the husband, Greg, asked that he be first. He wanted to sit in a room that held special meaning for him, but not where I would be doing the readings for the guests. This was fine, as I allow the clients to be where they are comfortable. As I entered the room, he asked if I felt any energy. I immediately was drawn to a corner where I saw an antique piece of furniture. I said this was his wife's grandmother's furniture, and she was making her presence known. As we continued to talk, he deeply wanted to connect with his mother. He had hoped that I would immediately feel his mother's presence in this room, as this was where he felt her presence. Again I was drawn to the antique mirrored dresser. I pointed at it, and said his mother was continuing to point at this same piece of furniture, and there was a connection that was hers. I asked if he was positive that his mother did not have some sort of attachment to it. Greg said they had other pieces of furniture in the house that was hers—but nothing in this room. He then went silent, and I could see the beginning of tears. There was a bench that was part of this mirrored dresser set, and his mother had reupholstered the cover. As he pulled the bench out and placed it in front of him, and alongside of me, he explained how she had redone the material on this bench. I could see his mother's energy, and she took her place, sitting on the bench directly in front of him. She talked about how it was one of her favorites, as the colorful red cherries on the material were how she felt: bright and cheery.

Greg had totally forgotten that she had replaced the bench's material. He was very happy that he was shown this piece of furniture, and how she helped him realize she did the work on this bench. He was also happy to know that she was there in the room. As his mother continued to speak, I could feel the tingling in my neck that was reminiscent of one of the symptoms of the illness she had before she passed. It was important for him to know that although it appeared outwardly that she was in intense pain, and she had not been able to speak for a period of time, she was now at peace. She also helped him realize he was not to worry about other events happening in the family, as they would take care of themselves. He had felt responsible for bringing closure to some of these things, and this gave him peace, knowing that his mother didn't want him worrying about some areas in his life.

Greg asked how he could continue to remain connected with his mother. I could see her overlap her energy with his, and knew she was reaching out and giving him a hug. Then she stood back and held her hand up. She said she was busy in heaven, giving energy out and helping others. As she reached out, I could see the rays of light emit from her palms in a love beam that she was directing at him. As I faced the palm of my own hand two feet from his chest in the same manner that she was showing me, I asked if he could feel her light. He acknowledged that just as I was opening my hand toward him, he felt a deep pulse of heat move into his chest. I told him that was not me, but rather his mother, who was directing this beam of light to him. She was sending her love. She also asked that I tell him she hugs him often, and she hoped he would feel these hugs along with the warmth of light rays to his heart.

When the reading was done, he asked if he could have a few moments to compose himself, as he was deeply touched by the presence of his mother. As I left the room, I thought, *This is what I am meant to do.* Seeing the healing messages and love that can be shared between loved ones, and between the energies of earth and heaven, makes me deeply grateful.

## The Ringing Phone

During a reading with sisters Nancy and Beth, we experienced some uncontrollable interruptions when Nancy's phone kept ringing. Nancy and Beth had scheduled the reading in order to connect with their mother who had died recently. Nancy lived in my neighborhood, but we had never met before, so she was surprised when she heard about me through a friend of a friend of an acquaintance. This chain of events in how Nancy found me were validation for her, that her mother had a hand in getting her to my door. As we began to talk more, Beth's cell phone rang. She reached into her purse and put the phone on silent, or so she thought. Five minutes later, her phone rang again. This time, she pulled it from her purse and saw that it showed "Number Unknown." She was both embarrassed and frustrated by the interruption, and told her sister that she did not know who was trying to reach her, but she would turn the phone off. She showed the phone to her sister to prove it was off.

I laughed at the interruption, and said that sometimes a phone ringing is affirmation of the message or the connection that is being made. Perhaps it was her mother trying another way to solidify all the messages she was giving them that day. We continued the reading, and once again Beth's phone rang. She was mystified. She turned to Nancy, and both validated that she had indeed turned the phone off. They double-checked the phone before Beth placed it back in her purse. I suggested that we acknowledge that it was her mother trying to reach her. I told her to make sure she checked her messages later. We finished the reading without further interruption. As they left, they were still talking about how weird it was that her cell phone would not stop ringing. She looked at it, and whoever had been trying to call had not left a message.

Three or four weeks later I received a phone call from Nancy. She reminded me of their reading where Beth's phone continued to ring even when it was shut off. She said nothing was wrong with the phone, and even though no messages were left on it that day, upon my urging, Beth had decided to check her messages a few days later. Sure enough, there was an old message that her mother had left her prior to her passing. Beth had never heard that message, and was in awe as to how that would have happened, as she is so diligent with all her calls and messages. I was happy to hear that Beth had heard the phone message from her mother, as well as all the messages and love that they experienced while at my reading. It was once again validation for them that their mother was very present in their lives, and through that unexpected message, they were able to validate the closeness they continued to feel with her.

I was doing some energy work at a friend's home in Sedona, Arizona. My friend's business partner had died earlier that year, and the partner's phone number had been disconnected for quite some time. A physical phone was still connected in the house, but with no active carrier. As we were doing our energy work in the backyard, we acknowledged the energy of my friend's business partner, and no sooner had we finished our acknowledgment than we heard the phone ring in the house. My friend went inside and picked up the phone. Nothing—not even a dial tone. We laughed, knowing that we had just received validation that his partner had acknowledged the energy work we were doing. It was an unexpected but much appreciated message.

Many of my clients are able to make a connection with those they have known in this lifetime, but sometimes the connections can be with loved ones they did not know at all. They may have a grandparent reach out to them, and although they may never have known that grandparent, the grandparent knows them. This could also be an older sibling that died prior to a client's own birth, but nonetheless, they are able to connect.

Alise made an appointment and drove a great distance to meet me face-to-face, rather than do the reading over the phone. As she entered my office, I sensed her grandfather. He patiently waited for her to ask all her many questions, as both he and I understood she was there to gain insight on her home life, career, and future relationships. Alise was definitely at life's crossroads, and I could hear her grandfather's message that this was important information. If he felt that she did not understand something, he would urge me to repeat or restate the information. Often, he would request that I tell her to write it down. He was guiding her on her journey. Finally, after he insisted on being a message-giver without identifying himself to her, I asked her if she had known her mother's father, as he was present and very much involved in all the information coming to her.

Alise was very surprised, as she did not know her grandfather, who had died before she was born. She did, however, acknowledge that her mother would continually tell her that she was very much like her grandfather in her facial features and mannerisms, and how her approach to life events were so much like his. Her mother believed he was with her, guiding and watching out for her. Indeed he was. Even though this woman did not know her grandfather, he was still very close to her, and his energy was very much a part of her life. It was not who she had expected to connect with on this day, but was very pleased to know that her grandfather was helping her. Alise could not wait to call her mother, and validate what her mother had been saying for many years.

Months later a woman made an appointment. As we began her reading, I acknowledged her father that had passed and now wanted to talk to her. I also needed to acknowledge that his energy felt very familiar. I asked if I had ever done a reading with her before, and she said no. We continued, and later during the reading, she asked a question about her daughter. The father told me he was watching over this woman's daughter, and not to worry, as she was very like him and he understood her quite well. Finally I made the connection: this was Alise's mother, and the man was Alise's grandfather. It was a welcome surprise, and again validation that this grandfather was assisting Alise on her journey. It brought great peace and joy to this woman, who deeply loved and trusted her father.

## When Suicide Occurred

Many clients look for answers to questions that have gone unanswered due to a death in the family—or in one such case, unfiled paperwork. Suicide is difficult because unless a letter or message is left behind, loved ones are often left not knowing why. They also feel guilty for not knowing or not taking action of some sort. A connection may often help bring some closure.

When Mary entered my office, I could sense she was very nervous. I asked the angels to come in and help her so she would be open to hearing all the messages she was meant to hear this day. Her father had died, and I could feel his presence, but another man also joined us. He stood off to the side and would not face me. I knew this man was important to her in this lifetime, but also sensed he was not a husband, but perhaps a man that she had deeply loved. He was not moving, so I knew that he had information for her.

She wanted to focus on her father, and other guides or angels that were present. Her questions were directed around her family, career, and future. This man waited patiently for all her questions to be answered, as he continued to stand with his back to me. I gently asked if she knew of a man that had recently passed from a self-inflicted gunshot wound. She bowed her head and said yes, this was a man she had loved very deeply who had committed suicide by shooting himself. He had done it outside the home so as not to create additional pain for the family. A family friend had found him, and she believed he had timed it so that she would not be the one to find him. She felt immense guilt because he had requested to see her the day prior, but she had said no. She was carrying this guilt— and it was time to let it go. He was insistent on being present to answer any of her questions. I heard him say that the important papers were in a stack of papers in the house. When I told her, she grew silent. I waited for her to ask questions. However, she said, "I fully understand, and thank you, I will look for them there. We had been looking in another place." She wanted to know if she had visited him, would it have changed anything. I heard distinctly, "No." He then proceeded to again talk about the papers, and began to show me stacks and stacks of papers. She agreed that there would be many stacks of papers, but he insisted on telling her exactly which stack to look in.

After she left, I never heard if she had indeed found that important information. I believed she would find the missing paperwork, as well as a letter that would answer many of her questions. I am not sure that this session left her fully at peace, but I do believe it brought some closure to some unanswered questions, and perhaps information that would help in bringing the closure she was looking for a bit closer.

It was also a very healing time for this man, because as he was able to let her know where this paperwork was, he turned to look at me. I sensed he felt bad for leaving unanswered questions, and was distraught that his loved ones were not able to find this information—meant to help those left behind in his life.

# Chapter 5

# Past-Life Ties

I t is impossible to validate that we have lived past lives. If you believe you have, it is equally impossible to validate events that you were involved in, created, or experienced. It is often difficult to validate behaviors that you have developed from those events or experiences. Because of the desire to validate information during readings, many intuitive readers refrain from opening this door and seeking this information. It may be that the intuitive is analytical in this area, and desires venues that have more validation principles, or it may simply be that the psychic or the intuitive is not called to do this work.

I do believe we have all lived many lifetimes, and I work with my angels, guides, and other energies for assistance here. This was something I did not intentionally focus on during my readings, but I quickly began to notice doorways opening, and information coming to me that would cause me to stop and ask for what purpose this information was being shown to me. There was a time when I wanted it to stop, and found I was not able to stop it; rather, I was directed that it had a purpose. This was a purpose to help heal, or help us understand events or experiences in this lifetime. If no purpose exists for seeing a past lifetime, then I do not see it. We are life learners, and if we can learn from an experience in a previous lifetime, we are able to open that door and obtain that information. I believe that many people in this lifetime are recognizing their knowledge or gifts from previous lifetimes.

The term *old soul* often is related to someone that has lived many lifetimes. *Young soul* is used to describe those believed to have lived few lifetimes. I believe that these terms are related more to the experiences your soul has had, versus the number of lifetimes you may have had. In each lifetime, we experience life and events in many ways. You may be a soul that has lived many lifetimes, but your experiences were similar in each. You may not have experienced the same depth of those experiences as another soul that has lived the same number of lifetimes. It is how we experience the events, the depth in which we experience them, not the number of times we experience them, that defines our soul as young or old. The terms then become irrelevant.

Many belief systems exist about the meaning or the value of our learning about our lifetimes. Although it is true—that it is impossible to validate any information you may hear from a reader about a past life—I believe we have reasons for specifically seeking information about our past lifetimes. Many times in the readings I do for clients they do not expect to hear information about a past life. If a past lifetime pertains directly to an event they are experiencing in this lifetime, they will get information about the past life. Spirit will continually provide this information to me until the client hears and understands the information. If I am meeting with a client, and I am shown information about the client's previous lifetime, I will ask my guides why I am seeing this. It comes to me as either seeing or hearing information about the client. I may see them living in a certain time period, experiencing an event, or physically in a location. I will sense or feel emotions from that lifetime as a method to tie lifetimes together or to assist in explaining what may be happening or manifesting in the present lifetime. I have clients that have memories from events that are related to present-day life events, ties to people or actions in this lifetime. This often helps explain why we are acting in a way that we do not understand, or why we have a feeling that we cannot define or get rid of. We may meet people that we believe we know from the past or be drawn to a location for no known reason.

When we open our minds to all the potentials and possibilities in the universe, we are not limited to this lifetime. Our souls have many lifetimes of experiences and memories. How open we are to these experiences provides another doorway for us to explore the depths of who we are.

## Danielle's Fears

I recently did a reading for a very wise twelve-year-old. She was extremely nervous, as this was the first time she had ever experienced an intuitive reading. She asked her mom to sit in during the reading, and they both asked if I was fine with this. I told them it was absolutely fine, as the messages come quickly. Perhaps quite a bit of information was going to be given, and it was the angel's way of saying that they might want to have two people listening. Danielle pulled out her list of questions, but before she could start, I was hearing that she was soft-spoken and nervous about speaking in front of people, and that she had a project coming up that would require her to speak in front of her class. Two angelic beings were there to help her through this challenge. She was to know that all was going to be OK, and they would be with her during this challenge. Danielle was staring at me. She simply said, "Cool," and then explained that there was special work she needed to do in her social studies class, and it involved speaking to her class. She did not want to do this, and was avoiding the assignment, not even mentioning it to her mom. Many people have a fear of speaking in public, but I was shown a glimpse of the basis of Danielle's fears. Her fears went beyond simply this lifetime. Many of our fears stem from events in our past lives. For Danielle, I could quickly sense that in many of her previous lives, she was required not to speak. She had a number of lifetimes in which she was punished for speaking out. Her soul needed to hear that in this lifetime, no one was going to harm her.

Before I could deliver this message, I needed to check with her angels and guides that it was OK to deliver this information.

She was an amazingly aware young woman, and was ready to both hear and understand this message. In this lifetime, she would be allowed to speak freely. These speaking assignments in her class were opportunities for her to learn that she was safe, and would not be judged or harmed by speaking up. Since she was still very young, she had not had the opportunities to do much public speaking, so each time she needed to speak up in the classroom, it brought her a sense of overwhelming fear. I was told by the loved ones around her that they were there to help and guide her. She smiled, and said she now fully understood why she had this fear. She was very intelligent, and I expect that she will do very well with future public speaking or simple classroom speaking events.

Sometimes our souls just need to hear that what we are experiencing is normal, based on something in our past. We carry memory of those past experiences in our bodies and in our DNA. We do not understand why we do things we may call silly or have no foundation for; we just do them. I see clients that want to release or let go of those things that hold them back. They search for answers to those behaviors or beliefs, knowing they are tied to something greater than their present life, but they are not quite able to get to the bottom of what it is.

## Sarah, the Worrier

Such was Sarah, who asked about everyone else in her family, but had no questions about her own life. Her guides were directing me to quickly answer her questions about her family while maintaining appropriate boundaries, so I would not be intruding in their lives. The guides were then urgently pushing me to ask Sarah about what she needed to focus on. I was hearing that she was self-sacrificing her life, trying to fix everyone else's life in a time where they did not want or need her to fix anything. This tie was so deep that she felt responsible to the point that she worried they would die. She said she worried frequently about them dying. She did not understand why she was so obsessed with it. This was why all her questions were about her family members, and none about herself. I told her that her family members were on their timeline exactly where they should be, experiencing what they needed to be, and she neither could nor should do anything to change that. I was shown a quick glimpse of a few lifetimes where Sarah had been responsible for many lives. In one lifetime, a mass death occurred on her watch. I explained this to her, and told her soul that in this lifetime she was not responsible for the lives of people around her. She could be comfortable in loving them and enjoying them in her lifetime, without feeling responsible for them.

We often have energetic ties to a past life, and our loved ones, guides, and angelic beings are here to assist us move beyond that, so we may live this life to its fullest potential. They remind us often that we are here to experience life, and not to fear it.

## Considering Remarriage

Many times clients ask if they have known their spouse in a previous lifetime. Sue's husband had died a number of years ago, and she was entering into a new marriage when she came to see me. She wanted to make a connection with her husband, and thank him for bringing this new man into her life. She began to explain the synchronicities in her life that caused her to meet this man, and with so many twists and turns in her story, I could not help but believe a higher hand was involved in making this meeting take place. It was about being in the right place at the right time (in the middle of a snowstorm) that these two found solace and friendship. This friendship later turned into a greater commitment when they moved forward with marriage. Sue had first decided not to attend the event that night, but at the last minute she went, rather than sit home alone. She felt that she had been pushed out the door. Also, she took a different route, and to this day she does not understand why, other than someone else must have been steering the car. She was not familiar with the road, and it took her longer than she had planned. She thought about turning around and going back home, but felt she was closer to the event than home. When she walked in, the event was near its end and the room had already begun to empty. She sat down in a chair to warm up a bit before going back out into the snow. This man, her future husband, sat down next to her, and they began to talk. When Sue replays that evening, she believes it was her late husband who pushed her out the door, took her on the wrong country route, and purposely led her to being late. Had she not attended, or had she been there on time, she might never have met this man. She was very grateful.

Sue then said that even though she was at peace with her first husband's passing, she felt that she had known her new husband in a previous life—when she met him, it was like talking to an old friend. I do believe that Sue reconnected with a loved one from her previous lifetimes, and that in this lifetime, her first husband had a hand in bringing them together, and continued to watch out for her.

At a recent open house where I was doing readings, I met Adele. She had come to this event with a friend only because her friend's sister had canceled at the last moment. She was extremely happy that she could fill the spot for a private reading with me. I sensed that Adele was very intuitive herself, and I asked how she was using her gifts. I saw two light beings standing behind her, and they were telling me that her gifts were true. However, Adele was overanalyzing the messages, and then convincing herself it was all a mind game, and nothing was real. I sensed through the energy of her body that she was not sleeping well, and wondered if she knew why.

Every night at exactly at 2:00 a.m., Adele was being awakened by energies that were moving through her house. She was not afraid, did not feel threatened, and felt they were just moving through. I asked her if she felt she had a portal in her home. I was seeing a long hallway with perhaps her room at the end. This portal, or opening, was an exit point for those people that had died, and were now moving into the light of heaven. Adele validated this. She sensed this was why they were coming there, but she said that this also happened in her last three homes. She did not think it was the home itself, but rather wondered if they were following her.

I was shown Adele in a number of previous lives where she was a shaman, a priestess, and a ceremonial master that helped people cross over into the light. Her soul had done this many, many times, and in this lifetime, even though she was not consciously doing this, spirits were still finding her—looking for assistance in crossing over. I asked Adele if she was OK with this, because she could say no in many ways. She could either completely close down the portal, or she could declare when it was open and when it would remain closed. She needed to get a solid night's sleep, and not continue to spend her nights sitting awake at the end of her bed.

Adele understood her role in her previous lives. By my simple mention of this gift that she had, she then understood why these spirits were coming to her. She also quickly made the connection with the time of night, and why it abruptly started at exactly 2:00 a.m., which is when the veil is at its thinnest. I told Adele it looked like they were waiting at the door, and when 2:00 a.m. came they were ready to move through. As we finished our session, Adele thought perhaps just one night a week she would help these spirits, but on all other nights she would ask them to go elsewhere and allow her to sleep.

When we moved into the house we live in now, we had a similar occurrence. My then thirteen-year-old daughter was not able to sleep soundly, and would wake in the morning feeling as if she had not slept all night long. She complained of aches and pains, almost as if her body were that of an aged person. She also insisted that I was moving things around on her shelves in her room. I was not, of course, and the shelves were too high on the walls for the cats to reach them without knocking the entire contents down. Each night, we looked at the figurines on her shelves to see where they were, and in the morning we would look at them again. Some days nothing would have moved, and on other days a few of the figurines would be in totally different places.

I checked in with my angels and guides, and heard that these were not our loved ones visiting, but rather the spirits of those passing through as they crossed over. My daughter had many abilities that she had used in a previous lifetime that would assist the aged, ill, or those that needed assistance in crossing over. In this lifetime, as a young girl she had not made the conscious decision to utilize this gift, yet those looking for help were finding her. I asked a friend to come help sage our house (see below) and close this portal. This allowed those seeking help and assistance to go somewhere else, and not seek out my daughter to help them. If they did not move on, they would linger in my home, and the energy in that area of the house would become heavy. My cats would sit at the top of the stairway and meow for what seemed like hours at a time. The closing of the portal was important for those that had died and were seeking help, the curious cats, and my daughter.

Those seeking help needed to move on and find another helper. For my daughter, it allowed her to sleep, and not take on energies that were not hers. At some later point in her life, if she desires to utilize these gifts she may do so, but for now she is content to sleep soundly and let them pass by her. She speaks very logically about this time in her life, and how these simple actions allowed her to get some sleep.

As we began the saging process, I called in Archangel Michael for protection and support, as well as Saint-Germain and Archangel Raphael for protection and assistance in clearing and closing this space. Saging is a process used by the Native Americans to protect and clear. You burn white sage, and allow the smoke to move about a room along the corners, walls, and windows. We said a prayer of protection and love, and asked that the portal be closed until such time as my daughter was old enough and knowledgeable enough to open it, if she so desired. The house was quiet that night, and has remained so since. A few times over the years we have saged the house again, but we have not been required to purposely close a portal to restore peace. My daughter sleeps well and now wakes feeling rested. Since we have experienced this in our own home, and I with my own child, I understand when I am approached by other parents with a similar concern for their child. I understand the fear, or concern, especially for those parents that do not have the knowledge of what to do, or who to contact for help.

## Young Justine

Some parents do not necessarily want to close off or stop these visitors from visiting; they just want to understand them. Often, they want to know who the visitors are, and if they will be safe if the visitors continue to be there. Justine attended one of my energy circles. At the end of these circles, I am open for any questions from the participants. Justine asked about a room in her home where her youngest daughter slept. Her daughter would often wake in the middle of the night and tell her mother there was someone in her bedroom. Justine, very intuitive herself, did not want the energy to go away. She just wanted to understand who the energy was. When I asked Justine why she wanted this energy in her home, she said that the room felt so good. It was a room in the home that people were drawn to for no apparent reason—they would just feel very good in that room.

I was able to tune in to the room as I asked for guidance from the energies. I asked Justine if the layout of the room would be such that as I entered, the bed would be to my right. If I moved into the room a few steps and turned to my right, I would be standing at the foot of the bed, looking at the headboard. She validated this information. I then told her that as I continued to face the bed, the corner to the left of the headboard felt like the strongest point where the energy was. She confirmed that this was the area most people were drawn to.

The energy I felt in this room was a motherly/grandmotherly one with immense healing energies. I called her the healer woman. The healing energies would include healing of the heart during times of great loss, illness, or death, and other losses people may have experienced. Other energies were drawn to the healer woman to help them in their healing in these areas. The little girl was being awakened when others would come to visit the healer woman. I did not feel the healer woman was there all the time, just when she was needed or asked to be there. I felt that if Justine closed the portal, the healer woman would remain, but the visitors would no longer come to her. This would allow her daughter sleep, but allow the energy of this healing being to remain in the home if they desired.

I asked Justine if she want to remove the energy and close the portal, or just close the portal. Both were her choice, and both within her ability to accomplish. She also had the choice of moving her daughter to another room in the home and converting this room into something else. She was very intuitive, and perhaps this could become a healing room or meditation room. She told me that she would close the portal by using sage and the angels to assist. If there continued to be nights that her daughter was not able to sleep, she would ask the healer to find another location to do her work. I asked the angels to assist Justine in this, and provide any support she might need. When Justine left the group that evening, she said she felt very much at peace, and had a deeper understanding of what she needed to do. I do believe this was the angels helping her already.

## Alexis Has Many Questions

Sometimes we have physical sensations that may be related to a past life, or we may hold fears that are memory-based in our DNA or aura. Such was the case for Alexis. She came to me with a very long list of questions, and wanted full details for each of the answers. As the angels and guides spent time answering her questions, I felt there was a greater reason for Alexis to be sitting in my office this day. It was time for the angels to ask Alexis a question. I needed to ask Alexis how well she was sleeping, but instead, the words that came out of my mouth were: "Do you know why you sleep with the lights on?" Alexis stared at me. I waited for more information from my angels, but when none came, we sat in silence and I watched her eyes begin to well with tears. I know that when this happens the angels have a reason for calling forward this information, and it is a healing moment for the client. It is usually an opportunity to let go of or release a memory or fear that is no longer needed in this lifetime.

My focus was now on Alexis, whose story was playing out from a previous lifetime. A large cloth bag that had once held grain was thrown over her head. She was being lifted and carried downward into an area that I called the dungeon, and it felt like we were in the lower levels of a castle-like structure. Even though it was midday, and the sun had been shining brightly outside, I saw very little light. I watched as this young woman was placed into a small room that was no larger than a crawl space. Filthy wet straw covered the dirt floor. I felt the sudden coldness rush through my body, and an understanding that she was being locked into this small space, closed off from the world above by a heavy door that shut out any light from the sunshine above. Once she pulled the sack off her head, she would be in total blackness.

Fear rose up in my own stomach, and I pushed back tears. I asked my guides to please stop this visual, these feelings. I did not want to go forward. I was told to keep going and reassured that all would be OK. We had gone from Alexis asking very simple questions about her job, new home, and family, to this information about a past life. She had not asked for this information, yet here it was, and I had no choice but to explain what I was seeing.

I asked Alexis if I should proceed into the past life, for it contained information about why she had this fear of blackness. Alexis agreed to continue. She was very curious, but I was the one seeing the dungeon and smelling its stench. I asked my guides for what purpose should Alexis know this information, and again asked if I could please stop experiencing this dungeon. The purpose for Alexis to know about this past life was to bring understanding about her fear of darkness. To have her understand why she was so fearful of the dark, she needed to hear about this past lifetime—and know that in her present lifetime she is safe. I explained what I was seeing and feeling. She was being punished for stealing in the market, and was put in this room with no light, where she was forgotten.

I explained that in this lifetime she probably had a fear of the dark. She may have thought it was something that scared her as a small child, but her fear was not from this lifetime. Alexis said she never knew why she was so scared. She had always slept with the lights on; when she was quite young her family had given up trying to change this. Even after she went away to college, her roommates accepted and adjusted to her oddity. It did not matter if someone was in the room with her or not, she was afraid of being in total darkness.

Thinking I was done delivering my messages—messages so she could have understanding and healing—more information was waiting for Alexis. The smell of the dungeon was so potent for me, I wondered if it was this that was making my stomach turn or if it was the fear that still overwhelmed me. The understanding of my experiences began to flow into words, and I let go, and let the angels and energies take over and assist with explanations. "Alexis, your fear of something biting you or crawling on you in the dark was also part of your past life. No rats, mice, spiders, or other crawling things will get you in this lifetime."

Alexis could not believe what she was hearing. She hated mice and had a fear of being bitten by one. The spiders she could tolerate, but she often felt that one was going to bite her. She told a story of going into a pet store with friends and having to walk out after she saw the mice and hamsters. She said it was not simply fear—she was worried that she would vomit. I asked her what odors bothered her, thinking it would be dirt, wet straw, or the stench of human sweat or body waste, but Alexis's answer surprised me. She hated *any* potent smells. In fact, she was overly sensitive to smells. She insisted that her roommates not use perfumes or heavily scented shampoos and lotions. She wanted absolutely no strong smells because she could not tolerate them. She often worried about getting headaches due to *anything* that smelled.

We paused in the reading to allow Alexis to absorb what she had just heard, and to allow her time to ask any questions. The angels and guides were quiet, but remained ready to answer questions or provide more insight. All Alexis could say was, "Wow, I get it." With the help of her angels and guides, and this information, she now had an understanding of her fears and low tolerances for darkness, rodents, bugs, and potent smells.

# Chapter 6

# Putting Up Boundaries

An amazing number of people in this world have gifts of intuition. Usually at every party or at some point during my week, I meet a person or hear a story about someone who feels he/she is intuitive, but due to fear or an experience that scared this person, he/she has chosen to block it.

One year I was asked do readings at a Christmas party. I was told that not everyone at the party would want a reading, but a steady flow of people were curious about what a psychic does, and what information could be available to them. The hostess asked me to introduce myself and talk a little about what I do, and how my gifts came about. She told me that her friend Clare was very intuitive, but was quite nervous about me being at this party. While I talked to the group, Clare would probably go outside or leave the room because it scared her so much to think of someone even talking about these connections. This was fine, as I believe if people are ready to have a reading or to hear any messages, they will be present. Otherwise, for whatever reason, including going outside, then they were not meant to, nor are they ready to hear any messages.

The hostess told the group that I would now speak to everyone, and nodded to Clare, expecting her friend to bolt for the door. I asked the angels to come in and help remove Clare's fear, and provide any information that would help her in whatever way they saw appropriate. Halfway through my explanation of the energies and what I do, I noticed Clare was still standing behind me, very near the door, but had not left. After I completed my introduction, the hostess took me to the lower level of the home where I was to do individual readings while the party continued upstairs.

Clare was the third person in line. She could recall seeing the energies of those that had crossed over. She did not know these people, but she saw their energy in white or rainbow colors. After her grandfather passed, she saw his energy standing in a doorway of her home, which both shocked and scared her. She had not slept that night, and for days after, she was afraid to be in her house, and would not allow anyone to leave her alone. Shortly after this scare she began to see shadows or gray, no longer in color or white. This frightened her even more, to the point that she did not tell anyone. I saw that her angels were helping her, and sensed it was important that she be able to discuss these events and her fears. I told her that I would teach her how to protect her home and her energy space so she could feel safe, and get back to sleeping at night without waking up scared. She wanted her grandfather to come to her, but she did not want to feel scared. She said that she was getting tired of not sleeping.

A few months after our reading, I checked in with Clare. She said that she had made many changes in her life, and often thinks about that reading. She still has moments of fear, and calls in Archangel Michael to wrap his wings around her or her home. If she feels she is being approached during the night by energies, she has the right to tell them to go into the light, and not to be in her home or around her. She has learned to shower herself with the white light of the divine, and only allow energies of the light to be in her home, which includes the energy of her grandfather. Clare admits that these are new practices, and it takes daily focus to incorporate these into her life. Sometimes she forgets, but she is confident that she now has all the tools she needs to feel comfortable to both allow energies to come to her or block them. Clare said she no longer lies in bed with her eyes wide open, afraid to close them for fear something may come to her. She uses her practices, and can now crawl into her bed with confidence and feel safe that she is alone in her room.

This is a very common event, when we may see shadows or movement out of the corner of our eye. If we cannot explain it, often it scares us. If we do not know how to protect or place our boundaries, we may leave ourselves open for continued visits of what may be shadow energies, much like in my daughter's room, where there was a portal that we needed to close to help her sleep at night.

## Seeing Shadows

Recently I did a house clearing and blessing. Barb had been sleeping in her daughter's bedroom for over nine years solely because the girl was afraid of the shadows she felt she was seeing each night. My friend Cindy asked if I would clear and bless her friend Barb's house so that Barb could begin to sleep in her own bed. Cindy said she would help me with this process.

When I arrived at Barb's home, Cindy was already there. We stood in the kitchen for a moment so I could assess where the energy was coming from in the house. I brought rocks to help both Cindy and me ground ourselves. Cindy felt jittery in the kitchen area, sensing the increase in the room's energies. I had already prepared myself and remained grounded, but as I spoke with the family, I handed a few grounding crystals to Cindy. I often bring various crystals or stones that assist in the vibrational values in people. In this case, these crystals were to lower the vibrational values that were making Cindy feel jittery; in fact, her legs were shaking. We moved between the floors of the home, saging and clearing old energy. We spent more time in areas that felt heavy with energy, and noted that the sage seemed to burn faster, and billow upward as it was clearing and cleansing. When asked to assess energies, I felt that an open pathway was in the home that those that had crossed over were using. I blessed that area, above the open stairway, and asked that this portal be closed, and any energy requiring an exit point from this earth, and also needing extra assistance, go somewhere else to find it—and not use this location and this home. Once again, I went from room to room in the house. Among the crystals that I brought with me was a bag of amethyst I had collected on a recent trip to an amethyst mine at Thunder Bay, Ontario. These were powerful energy stones, and like most of my worker stones, they were ready to work in helping to protect and grid the room where we were now standing.

As I moved from room to room, Barb's husband told me that he often felt a presence in the master bedroom, and spoke of the energy they felt in their large walk-in closet. I did not want to sage that room and leave all their belongings smelling of sage, but they told me to go wherever I felt was needed. Handing the burning sage to Cindy, I entered the closet, only to be met by a soldier dressed in Revolutionary-era clothing. He told me he was a prisoner, and was under the watch of the husband of this household. I understood that the husband had guarded prisoners in a previous life. The energy of the prisoner had followed the guard into this lifetime. Thinking he was still imprisoned, he was confused with his passing, and needed to cross over completely and move into the light. I spoke with him, and called in angels and guides to assist in this transition. I encouraged this energy to move into the light. I felt his presence move onward. We completed our walk-through of the home, and everyone agreed that the energies felt clear and calm.

That evening, the solder came to me, saying he was not ready to move on. I told him to leave my space, my home, and also that he was not allowed to go back to the home where we had been that day. Months later I checked in with the family, and they still were feeling the soldier's presence. The husband now understood he needed to be firm, and discuss the crossing over with this presence that needed to move on once and for all—he was no longer allowed there.

When a presence is assisted in crossing over, I tell the families to no longer acknowledge it or its energy. In some cases the energy is removed, if the family or a person continues to think about or acknowledge the presence, it returns, interpreting this as someone desiring them to remain at that site. The homeowners need not to focus any energy on what was. This may be difficult because they want to tell others about their experiences. I suggest they not even do this, as it misleads the energy into returning. By the simple action of continued focus on the energy's removal, they are energetically drawing it back. This is the law of attraction—what we focus on is drawn to us.

## Clearing for a Seven-Year-Old

At the same Christmas party where I met Clare, the hostess asked if I felt any energy around her seven-year-old son. When he saw movement or heard sounds in the house or his room, he would ask if anyone else had seen or heard the same thing. She told of a time that a movement caught his attention, and he asked if the rest of the family saw the same energy sitting in a rocking chair. Often she heard the same sounds as her son, and felt that presences were in the home, but only her son had the ability to both hear these noises as well as see the energies as they came into the home. Their house had been built on an old homestead, and even though I felt it was not on a burial ground, Native American energies definitely were on this property. The hostess agreed that many of the energies had a Native American feel to them, and weren't bad energies, just startling to the family.

I gave her some techniques to help clear his room, and draw protection around her son with the help of Archangel Michael. When I was packing up to leave, her son asked if he could have a white selenite stone that I had brought. Selenite is also a protection stone, and can be used to grid a room or area for protection. Of all the stones I had with me that evening, he chose this stone—without knowing anything about it, or its energy vibrational value.

## Rose and Daughter Elizabeth

Children are usually very open, so their ability to connect is easy. Without education or knowledge, what they are experiencing can be quite scary for the entire family, but it does not have to be. Many parents do not know who to turn to when their children have these experiences, or have questions about the sounds they hear or the energies they see. This was the experience of Rose and her daughter Elizabeth. When Rose contacted me, she asked if I thought it would be beneficial for her daughter to meet with me, or if it would scare her more to talk about what she was experiencing. I asked Rose to explain a bit more about what Elizabeth was experiencing. Elizabeth would see energies of people that had crossed over, but she was not able to decipher who they were or why they were coming to her. She had recently talked to her pastor, and though the pastor had truly tried to help, he admitted that he was just not experienced enough to guide her with all that she was experiencing. He told her to stay away from a Ouija board, and if she was afraid, to say prayers for protection—both very valid and useful. But Elizabeth still had questions as to who these people were and why they were coming to her.

Parents often ask if I can speak to their son or daughter. They usually are not sure what to ask me, but the conversation most often leads to a simple request to speak to their child. On this occasion, Rose made an appointment for her daughter. The evening of Elizabeth's appointment, I was met at my door by a smiling thirteen-year-old and a wide-eyed mom. Elizabeth said she was excited to meet with me. My son joined us in the entryway, carrying an animal spirit guide book, and I know that both of us were seeing the same dog. He asked if it was OK to explain what he was seeing, and proceeded to tell this mom and daughter that a dog was with them. As he explained the meaning of a dog spirit guide, Rose and Elizabeth exchanged glances. Rose said their dog had just died a few weeks earlier. When my twenty-year-old son asked if it was a German shepherd, Elizabeth said yes. This dog wanted both mother and child to know he was there as much for protection as for his love of them, and he was not far away.

I invited Elizabeth into my office, and her mom waited in my formal living room. Elizabeth immediately began to talk about these energies or shadows that she would see. She asked who was around her, and I sensed a great-grandmother. Elizabeth was only four or five when her grandmother died, and knew very little about her. She had a lamp in her room that had been her great-grandmother's, and its light would sometimes flicker or dim. This was indeed the great-grandmother, and even though someone had looked at that lamp's electrical plug, it continued to dim once in a while. Elizabeth validated this.

A particular energy would join Elizabeth when she played the piano, and I immediately felt his presence. I told Elizabeth that he was telling me how much he enjoyed her music, particularly when she played "Piano Man." She laughed, saying it was one of her favorite songs, and she played it often. She could feel his presence behind her while she played; sometimes it bothered her, and other times she was agreeable to him being there. I told her and him that he needed to ask for permission to be there, and if she felt uncomfortable, she had the right to ask him to leave.

Elizabeth talked about a number of energies, and asked why they were coming to her. I told her these energies were seeking her out for a couple of reasons. One, she could sense them, and they were able to get her attention; secondly, they were searching for help to move forward. I explained that if she wanted, she could ask them to move on and find another person that could help them, or she could direct them into the light, or she could ask for help from the angels, Archangel Michael, or Saint-Germain, to help them cross into the light.

Elizabeth was fascinated that I could see these energies. She had not been able to talk to someone that could validate that what she was seeing was not her imagination, but a true experience. As I would describe what I was seeing, she was also seeing it. This helped her know that what she was seeing, feeling, and sensing was very real. Children may be told by parents, friends, or loved ones that they have an imagination or that what they are seeing is not real. They may ignore or nullify the event, leaving the child to question if it is his/her imagination or if it is in fact an actual event. Elizabeth showed visible relief that she was able to talk with someone who understood and could put into words what she was seeing.

When Elizabeth asked why it felt like she knew places, we talked about past lives. As young as Elizabeth was, I wanted to understand her beliefs, and know how much she had told her parents. My guides shared that in previous lives, Elizabeth was not free with her gifts. In many of those lifetimes she was required to hide them, or was punished for a public display. In this lifetime, she would be able to use them publicly and be supported by family and friends, including her parents. They did not understand her gifts, but they were certainly open to supporting her.

Elizabeth said that she could talk to some friends, but with others, she had to be quiet. She had made the mistake of telling some friends that were not open or understanding of psychic or intuitive gifts. Growing up as an intuitive myself, I could understand, and could also remember some of my own experiences as a young girl and teen. Just like Elizabeth, I had learned with whom I could feel safe sharing information.

Elizabeth asked about tools such as tarot cards, or palm reading, but much like me, she would prefer to read a person's energy and communicate with the energies that had crossed over. She talked about the difficulty in hearing them, and not wanting to insert her own beliefs or words into messages or information. I assured her that she would understand this part of her gift better as she got older and was able to focus more on her gifts. Right now, she was young and needed to focus on school, homework, or family events.

Elizabeth understood this, and laughed because at times it was distracting to look at people's auras in her classrooms. She was very open to the message of focusing on the work in front of her, such as school, and then allowing other times where she could just focus on her gift. This is important to many young people because they need to focus on schoolwork, yet protect themselves from all the energy that is in the air during the school day. This energy includes all the collective energy of the student population, as their energy rises or falls from day to day.

If she interacted with a student that was depressed or sad, Elizabeth could be susceptible to picking up that lower-vibration energy. Without understanding the principles of energy, and how lower-energy vibrations are attracted to higher-energy vibrations as a means to balance the low vibrations, she could be drained of her own energy. This made sense to her, and she laughed, saying that she subconsciously knew this, but could not put into words what was happening. We talked about how to protect her aura and energy by thinking of a white light always draped over her. This would contain her own energy, and protect those lower-frequency energy vampires from tapping into her energy.

My own son hated the high school energy because he would pick up every low-energy vibration. He had a hard time distinguishing whether that low vibration was his or someone else's, so he just assumed it was *all* his. His last year of high school was done online because he needed to be away from the energy until he could learn and take an active role in protecting his energy field. By the time he entered college, he understood and could practice what he needed to do to both protect and shield his energy. He also learned when to shield and when to give energy to those that needed some additional energy, but he did this by choice.

Some very simple methods can be used to protect or create boundaries to shield your personal space as well as your home space.

# Chapter 7

# How to Shield

Susan, a frequent client, was familiar with the process of shielding, but needed a reminder and help with removing the fear. She had consciously shut down all her gifts when she was young. She believed then that she was not focused on the source of the energy. She tells me that she now understands, but when younger, she did not understand energy or the importance of working with divine energy, light, and pure energy. She believes she was perhaps mixing shadow energy. She says she thought this was a group that was using this energy in a negative way, and not for the greater good, or the greater purpose of those present. It was not of a godly, divine energy.

I first met Susan at an intuitive party, where I asked her if she knew she had a gift of intuition. She said yes, but that she was afraid of it—and did not want to discuss it. I could feel her fear so deeply that I wanted to help her shelter herself and remove the fear, but I realized that then was not the right time. After that first meeting, Susan came to a few of my group energy circles. She was very inquisitive and interested in the information that centered on making the connection with higher energies.

At recent private reading, she said she was interested in opening to her gifts if she had the right tools to protect and shield herself. Susan said there was a time in her life that she had felt a dark energy in her bedroom, and was unable to move. It was through prayers that she felt she was finally released from this energy, and from that point on had never opened the door to any potential connection. Most recently, she was drawn to work with these higher energies, but to focus on the divine energies.

# Angels and Ascended Masters

Calling in the angels is one way to protect your space or your own personal energy. Archangel Michael showed me this trick when we moved into a new home. I felt scared. I could not feel where the energy was coming from, nor could I predict when I would feel it, but it was most often between 2:00 a.m. and 5:00 a.m.—but not every night. The analytical part of my brain would try to understand why it was only on certain nights. I knew that the energetic veil was thinnest at that time. I tracked on the calendar to see if it was related to the new moon or full moon, or if it was related to any of the meditations I was doing, but there was nothing that I could correlate to my actions. Yet I kept feeling it was something that I was doing. Not for one moment did I think it was something I wasn't doing. Once I heard this message from my angels, I then asked them how I could protect myself.

Archangel Michael would talk to me about utilizing him to protect. It is his job to protect us and to take away our earthly fears, so why was it so hard for me to ask him for his help? Perhaps I felt others needed him more. He would laugh at this. He has the ability to be in more than one place at any given time, and therefore no one should feel that he/she couldn't call on him because it would take him away from someone else. Isn't that just like many of us who struggle to ask for any help, including that of the angels? How would I know how to protect myself, my home, or my family without being taught, and who better than the angel that says his job is to protect?

Archangel Michael tells us to ask this of him—as he wraps his *wings* around us, our children, our rooms, home, car, or whatever else we want to envision him protecting. He has a big capacity to wrap his angel wings, and I love to see him open and wrap them around everyone in my life. On these evenings when I would lie in bed with the pain of fear in my chest, I would ask Archangel Michael to please come to me, enter my space, and wrap his loving wings. I would see him do it as he worked his way from room to room, lovingly touching my children and protecting them.

He showed me how to envision him spraying his angel love in each room until there was nothing in that space but his love and protection. I would work my way from room to room envisioning him spraying this love in each, filling each room until the entire house contained nothing but his love protecting everything. No space was left for any shadow or dark energy.

Later, I would tell clients to think of Archangel Michael as a character from the movie *Ghostbusters*, with tanks on his back, moving from room to room spraying love and protection. White angel foam is what I would call it. My clients would laugh at this, but as they did, I would see him laughing also. He liked that I was spreading the word about his job of protecting us. The image that he gave me was something we all could visualize and allow him to do his work.

Other angelic beings or Ascended Masters that also assist in protecting us from energies that threaten to latch on to our energy source, and pull from it or harm our energies fields, include Athena, Archangel Raphael, Saint-Germain, El Morya, Ishtar, and Melchizedek.

Athena is best known as the Greek warrior goddess of wisdom, household affairs, and art and crafts. As the warrior goddess, she is known for her warrior spirit that protects, and also inspires women to proudly show their inner strength and courage. She encourages us to use our intuitive wisdom, and protects us while we do so. Ishtar is also a warrior goddess, and can be called upon for healing physical pain, as well as for protection from lower energies. I often catch Ishtar's stream of energy in photos, noticeable by her line of white light.

A number of years ago, when I was hiking in Sedona with a friend, we came to a place on the trail where I felt a dense energy and extreme sadness. I told my friend that someone had died there, and I needed to move the energy. My instinct was to call upon Archangel Michael, and as I did so, I felt another loving presence. Archangel Raphael identified himself to me. Archangels Raphael and Michael often work together to move energy or help remove negative energies from people or places. Raphael is known as the healer angel, and at my request he was joining us to heal this area. I could feel his loving presence, and later my camera caught his green light in lovely orbs and sparkles alongside Archangel Michael's blue light.

I often call upon Saint-Germain. He was a royal count of the French region whose real name was Comte de Saint-Germain, or the Count of Saint-Germain. Though involved in politics, he was multitalented in music, art, and languages. He also was a psychic, providing readings to many of the European royalty and high society. He spent time studying and teaching occult subjects and alchemy. He is said to carry a violet flame to transmit lower energies or to assist light-workers or others that want his help. He also provides guidance, protection, and courage, and is said to work hand-in-wing with Archangel Michael. I also often catch Saint-Germain's presence in my photos as a long line or ray of violet light.

Below are messages I received from Archangel Michael and Archangel Raphael, both asking that their messages be shared.

*Messages from Archangel Michael: My dear children, we are all afraid at times during our lives, when we do not have need to be afraid. It is my purpose to protect you and remove your fears so that you may enjoy a more fulfilling life. Do not be afraid that you are alone. Do not be afraid that something bad will happen to you. Understand that you are protected, and all is as it should be. You are perfect, and as the perfect being that you are, you are to be protected. I will be present for all of you; to love you, protect you, and remove any of the fears you have that you hold close to you. These held fears prevent you from truly living freely in this life. You are here to live freely. Allow me to remove any of the challenges, roadblocks, or fears that hold you back from being in joy and laughter. Fears that keep you from experiencing love. Fear from stepping into ownership of your own being. Let me assist to bring peace and love to your soul during this journey.*

*Michael wants you to know that to call on him, you may use the following:* Archangel Michael, I need your help. I ask that you be with me and protect me now.

**Messages from Archangel Raphael:** *I am also committed to providing protection in your lives. But I also commit to assisting in the healing of your heart, healing of your soul, and healing of any fear-based experiences you have from present or past. Let me assist in healing your soul from beliefs, behaviors, or judgments that may have held you back or continue to hold you back on this journey. For it has been your journey that has brought you to this point, and allowed you to come this far. Now, allow yourself to go further by accepting my loving and healing to clear the path. Continue on your path as you understand your light, your love, and your purpose here during the journey. Call on me when you are unsure of this direction. Call on me when you feel off path, for I will be here with you on this journey. I am here to hear you, heal you, and protect you.*

*To call Archangel Raphael:* Archangel Raphael, I need your help. Please come to me now and shower me with your healing light, love, and energy. Heal this situation with loving energy.

# Rocks and Crystals

After we had lived in our home for a few months, a friend visited. This friend worked with crystals and rocks, but also was doing work with sacred geometry and patterns of geometry in our world. Sacred geometry is the geometry used in the planning and construction of religious structures such as churches, temples, mosques, religious monuments, altars, and tabernacles, as well as for sacred spaces such as temenoi, sacred groves, village greens, and holy wells. It is also used in the creation of religious art. In sacred geometry, symbolic and sacred meanings are attributed to certain geometric shapes and geometric proportions. Aside from the ordinary use of counting and calculating, certain numbers have symbolic meaning. Plane figures, such as the polygons, triangles, squares, hexagons, and so forth, are related to the numbers (three and the triangle, for example), are thought of in a similar way, and in fact carry even more emotional value than the numbers themselves, because they are visual.

The study of sacred geometry has its roots in the study of nature, and the mathematical principles at work there. Many creations observed in nature can be related to geometry. For example, the chambered nautilus or mollusk grows at a constant rate, so its shell forms a logarithmic spiral that accommodates that growth perfectly without changing shape. Honeybees construct hexagonal cells to hold their honey. Many examples of sacred geometry exist in nature, and these are only a few examples seen by believers in sacred geometry to be further proof of the cosmic significance of geometric forms.

When I greeted my friend at the front door, she commented on the pile of accumulated crystals and rocks placed there. As I showed her around my home, she also noted the rooms that I had put amethyst in. She asked me if I had someone come to the house to purposely grid it in its sacred form. I did not understand what she meant, and she graciously gave me a quick lesson in her recent studies. No, I didn't have someone come and purposely place crystals and rocks in the rooms of my home and locations outside. But when she drew my attention to all the locations and the patterns that I had created, it made sense that I had been guided either from past life knowledge or by my guides, or perhaps by both. We both laughed at the synchronicity of it all. I would not call myself religious, but I am, however, very spiritual, and I do associate much of the work I do with nature. It would make sense that I would comfortably align the space I live and work in with the sacred geometry to allow a place of peace, love, protection, and connection with the energies of the universe.

Another method of protection that I recommend to my clients, especially parents, is to envision an immersing white light coming down over them or their children, much like you would envision water from a showerhead. This provides protection, and acts much like Teflon coating, in not allowing other, denser energies to enter our space. When my children were young, before I sent them off to school I would cover them in white light.

Many stones of protection are available. These are only a few of my favorites that I use, as well as recommend to clients when asked.

- Certain crystals such as smoky quartz and black tourmaline have the ability to absorb negativity and put out pure, clean energy.

- Fire Agate has a deep connection to the earth, and its energy is calming, bringing security and safety. With strong grounding powers, it supports us during difficult situations or events.

- Amethyst is an extremely powerful and protective stone with a high spiritual vibration. It guards against psychic attack, which is a negative-energy attack. Amethyst protects and transmits this negative energy into love.

- Angelite is said to be the stone of awareness for the New Age. This is an extremely peaceful stone, as it allows connection to the angelic realms while also providing protection for the environment or the body.

- Bloodstone heightens the intuition and increases mystical and magical energies while also having the ability to banish evil and negativity to direct spiritual energies.

- Jet is a powerful stone. It is formed from fossilized wood, but looks like coal. It has been uses as a talisman since the Stone Age. It is believed to draw out negative energy, and assists in alleviating unnecessary fears. When worn around the neck, it is a stone of protection, guarding against violence and illness, and provides protection during spiritual journeys. My son wears his jet carved in the shape of a bear, his animal spirit. I have put it in our family vehicles, and my daughter carries a large piece in her backpack.

- Obsidian is a powerful protective stone. It forms a shield against negativity while providing a grounding cord from the base chakra to the center of mother earth. It is helpful for highly sensitive people, as it assists in blocking psychic attack and removes negative spiritual influences.

- Smoky Quartz is one of the most efficient grounding and anchoring stones, while at the same time raising vibrations during meditation. It is a protective stone with a connection between all chakras and an anchoring of each to the base chakra.

- Tiger's-Eye is a stone that was carried as a talisman to protect again ill wishes and evil curses. It is said to be the stone of integrity, bringing out the correct use of power while assisting in accomplishing goals.

- Tourmaline heals cleanse, purify, and transform dense or lower vibrational energy into a lighter or higher frequency. It grounds spiritual energy, clears and balances all the chakras, and forms a protective shield around the body.

- Black Tourmaline is particularity effective in protection from psychic attack, spells, ill wishing, and negative energy of all kinds.

When my son started college, he told me he was having a hard time maintaining his energy levels. I could see his aura was filled with holes, and his personal energy was leaking beyond his own body. The bestowing of light was not working for him, and he was asking for another method to shield and protect his energy from leaving his personal space, but he was also asking for ways to keep others' energy off or out of it. I suggested a number of stones. For a while, he would carry them in his pockets, and I often found them in the washer or dryer, or in the couch cushions. Under seat cushions in our house, you would no doubt find rocks, not loose coins. He felt bad when he lost a stone, and I would find him looking through the rocks in my office.

At a local trading post, we found a handcrafted jet bear necklace that my son could not put down. He was drawn to and felt protected by the jet, as well as the bear totem carved in it. He would have slept in that necklace, but worried about it becoming damaged. It hung each night from his bed and I never saw him leave the house without it. Over time, he added other small stones to a growing string of necklaces and amulets he wore around his neck. I gave him a black tourmaline with a citrine quartz, and when the tourmaline broke in half, he continued to wear it that way, feeling that the energy the stone was protecting him from had actually broken it. I agreed with him. I too would wear various stone bracelets and earrings or put loose rocks in my suit jacket pocket before I'd leave for work each day. My stones were chosen due to what I was feeling the need to open up or close off. Some days I would welcome the energies, and others times I might want to shield myself a bit. I tell my clients that we all have the ability to say no. Once we protect ourselves or our space, we have the right within our energy fields to say no to psychic intrusions. I call this our personal security system.

Client Theresa hosted a party. When guest Bella sat down, I immediately sensed this was going to be a very different reading. She was quite guarded, and her energy felt almost stiff, as if slabs of cement were guarding her energy field. Most guarded was her heart. She asked analytical questions, and I was having a very difficult time connecting to her aura and her heart. I could see a young boy off in the distance by a fishing dock, with his back to me. He refused to turn toward me. He was angry, and I sensed he was trying to ignore the entire experience and my intrusion into his space. I instinctively knew this was Bella's son. I asked him to come and sit with us, and again he refused the connection. He was telling me that no one listened to him, and he was not able to do the things he wanted to do. He spoke of computers or electronic games, and moved to show me how he wanted to play these games, but could not. I asked Bella if during his lifetime he had been allowed to play computer or electronic games. She coldly answered that, like all young boys, he had played them in life.

Immediately I knew she was looking for something more solid as validation that this was her son, and I also sensed that it would be a very healing connection between mother and son. The young boy turned toward me, but stayed at a distance. He told me that he was angry because no one told him, and he had become very tired of all the medications and tests. He wanted them just to end, but they did not. He was showing me all the tubes and IVs that had been placed in his little body, and the pills and other medications he had endured. Tears welled up in my eyes as I felt his sorrow and pain. Bella told me that he had not had major treatment, and that they had told him everything as it was happening. She did not understand his messages, and was clearly not happy. I asked the young boy for more validation, again attempting to make this connection so the healing of the heart could happen. The boy turned his back on me, and once again I heard him say, "No one will listen." I repeated this message to Bella. She firmly said she did not understand this, and then asked if there was another child there with her son. Bella told me she had lost a second child. I could feel the presence of this infant, and he was under the watchful and loving energy of a grandmother.

Bella didn't seem especially happy with her time with me, and I felt a deep sense that something was just off. I sent love to Bella's family, and asked the angels to assist in any further healing that was needed. I finished with the other guests at the party and sat with the hostess after all had left. I expressed my concern over the experience with her friend, telling Theresa that I would provide additional time to Bella if she would like. I could not release the feeling that there was work yet to be done with her and her son, but for a greater reason beyond my understanding, I was not able to assist in the connection that evening.

My angels and guides continued to push me to learn more about this little boy. I knew if I did not pursue this, I would not be sleeping that night. I asked Theresa if I could ask her a few questions about the child, and learned that he had not known he was terminally ill until the very end of his life. His parents had wanted to protect him from this information so he could live carefree. His parents also tried every treatment available. The little boy had extensive traditional medical appointments and medicine, as well as holistic treatments or other alternative treatments. As a parent, I understood what would drive one to act and do as this little boy's parents did, and try all possible treatments—but not share what was happening so the child could just be happy and not worry. I also understood why Bella was guarded and appeared angry at hearing these messages. She wanted to know he was fine, and with this, bring some peace to it all.

Bella's son was fine; I could see him, very healthy, sitting on the dock fishing, basking in the sunshine. Every now and then he would dip his foot into the water and kick up a bit. He was healed, but he wanted her to know how he felt during that time. It was not meant to bring guilt or sadness, but rather to state simply this is what it had been. He wanted to be heard. His parents had acted in the best way they could at the time. The son acknowledged that and understood, but he was still angry. During the time of her son's illness, Bella did not tell friends and co-workers much of what was happening in her life. Co-workers were surprised how she had been able to remain focused and calm during that time, once they learned of her son's passing.

Thanking the hostess, I got into my car to drive home. I knew I was not done with this little boy. A few minutes into the drive, I could sense him sitting next to me in the front seat. He wanted to come home with me. I told him that I loved him very much, but his mother loved him more, as she was his mother. She loved him, and would continue to love him forever. I asked Saint-Germain to join me, and assist this little boy in getting back to the light.

I also told this little boy that he could not visit me, as his place was not here anymore, but rather in heaven. I told him again that his mother and father loved him very much, and he could send them love and visit them, as I knew both his parents would welcome a connection. I told him to look for his brother, and together they would be with family in heaven, such as their grandparents. When I sent love from my heart, I felt the boy's energy leave my car. I asked that Archangel Michael continue to protect me, and also protect this little boy's family. I knew I was complete once I had acknowledged the boy's anger at not knowing earlier how ill he was—and that he was going to die. He just wanted to be heard and for it to be acknowledged that he had not been happy with that decision. I also knew that he now understood why his parents chose not to tell him, and why they chose all the medical treatments he endured. It was only from a place of pure love. His anger was released, and in its place I saw the light of love for his parents. I slept very well that night, knowing that was exactly why his mom had come to the party, and I also knew that the angels would lovingly continue to work with her to help the healing process.

# Chapter 8

# Getting Out of the Way

Judy had had many private readings from me, and now had invited me into her home to do individual readings with her family and close friends. On this particular day, as her friends took turns meeting with me, I could feel the energy rise in the home. When Judy sat down across from me, there was a level of deep confidence within her. I could feel that she had an important request—and she did. She requested that she be able to speak to a specific celestial being: Jesus. This was the first time I was asked so directly to speak to a celestial being, and it caught me off guard. Often celestial beings will come into a session or reading. Now I understood her focus, and her level of confidence. She was firm in her request. I, on the other hand, was immediately flooded with feelings of fear and doubt, and was overwhelmed with many other emotions that were hitting me too fast and hard to really put names to all of them. Would I be able to do this? I sat back and took a deep breath. I felt as if I were suspended in time, almost as if this moment were surreal. Who was I to be able to make this connection for her? I was humbled.

I needed to take a few more breaths, and check where my ego was at the moment, and where my guides and angels were. I was quickly reassured that all would be fine. I could hear Archangel Michael telling me to trust, and just be in this moment and move aside. I felt this moment was a gift. I firmly held on to the rock in my hands that I use to both ground and connect me to the angelic realms. As my energy vibration level rose, I couldn't feel my feet or legs as I floated upward with the vibrational frequency. Then he stepped in, meeting me at a vibrational frequency. I asked Judy to allow me a moment to move myself out of the way so that he could be present for her. To this day, what I recall from that experience was I needed to move aside so the messages for her could be available without filters.

Later, I asked Judy if she would tell me about this loving experience and connection. Judy's messages reminded her that she was not in charge or responsible for others' healings. This helped her establish the needed boundaries. This visit from Jesus was confirmation that she is an agent for the Divine, but not responsible for anyone's beliefs or feelings about connections to the Divine. Those she might have been feeling responsible for must form their own beliefs, recognition, and connections, and she was to believe that it was acceptable to let go of trying to be responsible. Judy was also reminded how loved she is. An immense flow of light and love had enveloped the room, shrouding Judy in white light as he immersed her with love. He reminded her how easily she could access this love at any time. She had the capability to access and retrieve it, which Judy said provided an anchor that she uses often. She said she had felt comfortable with the angels since she was a child, but did not recognize how close they are to us, and that we all have the ability to connect with them so easily. Judy told me that she speaks to her angels often now, and senses their presence without having to physically see them. She believes she experiences them psychically and spiritually, acknowledges them as her "friends," and speaks to them more readily than in the past.

After her experience, Judy said that she has a more relaxed life, enjoying the natural flow of life and light, rather than trying to control the flow. Judy's reading validated what she had already known, but did not recognize. She now regularly relates to her angels and light beings, wanting and welcoming them to interact with her. Being in a natural flow of energy, she believes she is now more prepared because she openly relates to any of the angelic beings when they present themselves. She also feels comfortable talking about these experiences with others, as they have become such impactful contributors to her life.

On the evening when Judy invited me into her home, after I met individually with her, her husband, and her two married daughters, the family told each other about their experiences. Later, Judy told me what an incredible reinforcement that was for who they are as a family—and as individuals. This allowed them another way to validate for one another their spiritual and family journey together.

When such requests are made from a place of pure love, I believe that the connections are made with the assistance of guides, angels, and our loved ones. Judy's openness allowed this amazing energy to come forward for her to receive his messages and feel his love. This was a connection of validation and continuation for Judy and her family. These are opportunities for me to have a continuing deep gratitude for my gift, and are reasons why I need to use this gift with others. Doing so creates a ripple effect of love and energy.

## Sedona Experience

On a weekend trip to Sedona with two girlfriends, I experienced this ripple effect again. After a day of hiking, I was looking forward to having some quiet time that evening. Throughout our day, I had been exchanging voice mails with my friend Mark, who lives in Sedona and owns a spiritual tour business. He was busy with a large group that had come to Sedona with a well-known spiritual leader. My friend was providing guidance, and assisting the group when they were on the land and experiencing the Sedona energy with the vortexes. In one of his messages, he asked me to meet him at his house that evening to help facilitate any energy needs. The spiritual leader was doing some personal work on his own energy, and my friend believed it would be beneficial to have the two of us anchor, balance, and elevate the energies. Being guided to make myself available to help, I said yes. I knew that this energy was not only for the spiritual leader, but was to be the doorway for this energy to be shared with his group. This was the ripple effect that energy has, and I could see the impact it would have on the group he was leading as it rippled outward, much like dropping a pebble into a lake.

When I arrived at my friend's home, the energy was heavy, and I knew my work was to raise the vibrations so a higher connection could be made. As I stood on one side of the spiritual leader, the Divine Mother joined us on the other side. I stood in awe of her presence. Her love and the peace she brought to the room immediately enveloped all of us. I began to feel my own vibrational energy rise again. I stopped trying to analyze the energy, and relaxed, just allowing myself to be in the energy. I realized that I was helping balance the feminine energy, and in working with the spiritual leader and my friend, we were anchoring and elevating this energy.

I told those present that we had been joined by the Divine Mother, and she wanted to make her presence known for the work that was to be done that week through this spiritual leader. She was there at that moment to assist in this spiritual leader's transformation and release of energies. She was acknowledging him for the work he was undertaking, as well as the work he was to be doing in the coming year. It was important that he release old and allow these new, higher-frequency energies to become embodied within him. It was not for me to interpret, only to tell what the messages were, and try to put into words the immense love I was feeling. In this case, it was the removal of the physical energy that he held, and a replacement of pure love. As I felt the stagnant energy being pulled from his body, I was directed to help pull and release it to the heavens. As it finally trickled down to a narrow thread, it was quickly replaced by platinum light and love showering down over the leader and everyone. I explained what I was seeing, and what was happening; the words were not my own, but were being provided to me.

The leader requested a break. When he returned, the energies with us asked that he lie down, and as we moved him to a healing table over which stood a copper grid, we continued to hold the energy. The copper tubes formed a house-like structure over the table that moved upward above his head. As Mark and I stood opposite each other alongside the spiritual leader, I continued to express what I was seeing and feeling in the room. The spiritual leader's grandmother was now in, and messages of his childhood were revealed to him. As the spiritual leader continued his journey into his past, my friend and I were bathed in the silence of the energy. Abruptly, Mark whispered, "Laurie, what's happening?" We both felt the table, the grid, and the spiritual leader levitate as the vibration lifted higher and higher. I could not answer, as my focus was solely to hold the energy in the space, be a conduit for what was coming in, and be of any assistance that was needed to hold this high frequency. It was not my place to ask, nor know specifically what was happening, only to put trust in the angelic beings that were now busy at work. There would be time later to reflect on what we had experienced.

This was another example of where I was required to move out of the way and just be in the energy. This energy was of many light beings, celestial beings, and ancestors of this spiritual leader. I needed only to be in complete trust of this energy, what it meant, and for whom it was intended. I will never forget this night, and often think about it. Sometimes no words or labels exist for what this energy is or how it feels. It just *is,* and it is only meant to be within and experienced without having to understand or label it. This was certainly a time when I was required to put aside all beliefs and perceived limitations that I may have held, in order to allow what was meant to be, to happen. In doing so, I was shown new energies and new healings. The work that was to be completed by my being present had been completed. My gratitude continues.

Many times we do not fully understand what we are experiencing, and the messages, information, or energy may be solely for the purpose of healing. Often a client may ask about a friend who has passed.

## The Friend Who Passed in an Accident

At another intuitive party, many family members and friends were present. In her reading, Mary asked about a friend who had passed. I saw this friend sitting in a car, but she was turned sideways, not making eye contact with me. She was mad, embarrassed, or feeling guilty, and I was having a difficult time picking up which emotion I was feeling, as they all seemed to hit me at once.

The woman remained present—but silent. This indicated to me that this was a healing opportunity for this woman who had passed. As I asked for more information about the car accident, Mary said they did not really know what happened, other than this woman had taken a different route that night. When the woman turned to me, I learned immediately the source of all her emotions. It was winter, when it gets dark early. She had decided to take a different route for no other reason than she felt like it. She herself did not understand why. She was afraid on this road, and admittedly was going too fast for her driving experience, the weather, and the unfamiliar road. All created conditions for her to lose control of the car and be killed in the accident. She was angry—angry with herself, the road, the car, and the experience in general. She felt guilty for leaving loved ones behind, and missed them dearly. She wanted to apologize to her parents for being irresponsible in her driving, and for putting them through such pain as they continued to wonder what had happened and why she was on that road on that particular night. I saw the angels come in and surround her with love. She wanted to say that she was fine, and that all was as it was supposed to be. She had accepted how this had transpired, and understood that there was no blame, guilt, or anger that anyone needed to carry anymore. The healing around this moment was to release any held energy from the woman, which allowed her to move to a place of understanding and love.

She now turned fully toward me and asked me to thank Mary. Without Mary asking about her, and wondering how she was doing in the afterlife, she would not have been provided the opportunity to quickly move through her pain. This connection was all about the healing messages that needed to go to the woman's parents, and then being able to release her own energy that kept her from moving to the next level in her afterlife. Eventually she would have worked through this energy, and the angels would have stepped in to help. She would have gone on to her next level even without the reading with Mary, but it provided healing, and a method to quickly move through the energy she had been holding—and that was the difference. Mary promised to deliver these messages to the family, which would allow peace and closure on both sides of the veil.

In this event, Mary moved out of the way and allowed the messages to come to her. She held no judgment or beliefs as to how the information should or should not be. The communication could be open, with the energy for both Mary and the deceased woman to move forward.

# Chapter 9

## Listening to Messages

**M**any clients seek answers to lingering questions or to bring closure to something they have thought about and carried within them for quite some time.

Leslie contacted me because she wanted to connect with her mother, Ida, who had passed away ten years earlier. She wanted to apologize for being so angry at her mother for so many years. Leslie's memory of her childhood was that she had behaved very badly when she was sixteen. At that time, she had overheard an argument between her parents. Her mother was yelling at her father over his wanting to leave her, and take Leslie's sister with him—but not Leslie. Leslie became very angry with her mother, instead of being angry at her father. She never told her mother specifically why, but held this anger for years.

During our reading, Leslie was able to connect with and apologize to her mother. At first, Ida was confused about the apology, and told me there was nothing to apologize for. I could see the rays of white light Ida was showering down over her daughter. Leslie needed to tell her mother how she felt terrible that they never talked about what had happened. Over time, it had been one of those uncomfortable memories that became buried. Leslie also wanted to ask her parents if they understood why she was not able to have a relationship with her only sister. Both of her parents were able to tell Leslie that they understood about her sister, and there was nothing more she could do. Being able to have this conversation of closure helped to bring her a sense of freedom, and an understanding of all the energy she had carried around with her for many years—and she could let go of it now. Doing so allowed a huge heart opening to her mother, and a deeper understanding of the pain Ida may have felt at that time. This connection also helped Leslie look at her own daughter with different eyes and much more understanding.

Leslie wrote me that her heart has stayed open, and she also feels compassion for her sister, and understands that her sister cannot be any different from how she is. She feels the support and strength from her entire family. Being able to feel this has helped her keep her heart open and more accepting. She also feels a much closer connection with her guides and angels, and has let go of trying to be perfect in her spiritual quest—and to allow it to just be as it is. She mediates more, but only when she feels like it, as it no longer feels like it is something that she *has* to do. That feeling of *having* to do something kept her from meditating, and now she is freer to make that connection.

Leslie has attended a number of my intuitive circles, and I have seen the difference in her. Her heart has remained open, and she is well on her spiritual journey. Letting go of pent-up energy created space for her to fill with new, lighter energy that will carry her forward, instead of keeping her stationary or holding her back.

During the years that I have done readings and have helped make connections, I have found that the apology is really not necessary for those that have passed over; rather, it is for us still present here on earth. We hold energy for the things we forgot to say, or things we wish we would have said—and sometimes we hold unnecessary energy for the things we said and wish we had not. Our apology allows us to release energy we spend on wondering if or wishing we could make changes in something that happened in the past. At times, a client may apologize or ask for forgiveness, and I will hear a very firm response from his/her loved one: "For what?" I will feel the energy from the loved ones as confusion, or sometimes even frustration, because they cannot attach a memory to an apology or forgiveness. Some that have passed over become irritated that their loved ones here on earth have held on to that energy. We are not meant to hold bad feelings within us; these feelings are meant to be released. Feelings we hold keep us in a lower frequency, and rob us of our happiness and joy here on earth. Of course, our loved ones that have crossed over would want us to release any emotions that continue to keep us at a lower vibration, or those feelings that continue to give us emotional pain. If we are able to release these emotional feelings of pain, guilt, or sorrow, then we can move into a place of joy and happiness. This is where we want to be, and this is where our loved ones want us to be.

Sometimes we need to bring closure by understanding someone's passing in better detail. Or perhaps we left some things unsaid. This may happen when loved ones pass unexpectedly, and we did not have time to speak with them prior to their crossing. Or, our desire to connect may be due to their passing earlier than anticipated, and we thought we had time to tell them we loved them. Sometimes we simply want to know if our loved one made it to heaven.

## A Drowning Victim Connects

At an intuitive party for friends and relatives of a young man that had drowned, this happened. As a beautiful young woman with dark eyes sat across from me, I could feel a joyous energy move quickly to be near her. I could feel this young man's excitement, and asked the young woman if she had a brother or boyfriend who had passed. She nodded at me as tears began to roll down her face. The young man had been waiting to tell her that he was fine, and was well on his next journey. He did not want anyone to worry about him. He wanted her to see that he was happy and full of joy. I asked her if this was how he was in life; he was showing me this joy and happiness as a continuation from this lifetime to the next. He was so loving and full of joy, and was trying to send this loving, joyous, high energy to this young woman. She was his fiancée, and her question was whether she would ever find the kind of love that she had with this young man. She asked if she would ever get over the loss and be able to love again. He was saying *yes-yes-yes*. He wanted her to be happy, and to hear from him that it was OK for her to move on.

He was happy and moving forward on his new journey, and he wanted her to go forward in her journey. He knew she would never forget him, but he was telling her to ignore those in her life that were saying she had to wait before she could date. She nodded, and told me she understood this. She had dated another young man once, but heard feedback that friends thought it was too soon, even though it had been almost a year since his passing. She wanted to ask her fiancé if it was OK to begin dating again, and if he was all right with the person she had seen. He responded yes, and was happy she had chosen this friend. He reminded her that he was no longer on the planet, and that she did not have to wait. There were too many years before she'd see him again. He wanted her to be in joy, and if that meant dating and laughing and having fun, then he wanted her to do this.

She thanked me for the messages, and I reminded her to continue to speak to him directly, because he could hear her. He wanted her to give his mom a hug, and acknowledged that his mom was having a really hard time. Though he had not been the oldest child, as the only son, he had been the man of the house when his parents split up. His mom was desperately missing him, and he also wanted to send her love and let her know he was OK.

Sometimes clients want to know if their loved one was aware that they were with them, or if they were in pain. Being at my mother's side in her last days on this earth, I would watch her breathe. I would watch for any slight movement that might tell me if she was just sleeping, or in the deep coma that the hospice's care providers would mention. She was peaceful, and every now and then, I was certain I'd see a frown flutter across her brow. I would look for any of those familiar facial expressions, or anything familiar, but there was nothing. She was deeply in a different place, and the angels and guides were working with her, preparing her for the time when she would cross over. But she knew I was there, that all of us were there. Other senses were taking over for her, and she knew that she was surrounded by much energy that would cover her with love, whether it was of this earth or from beyond.

## Moving Back Home

Many times clients simply want to know who is with them, as they may feel a loved one's presence, but are not sure who it is. Mara was making a transition from attending an out-of-state university to one in Minnesota. She had been thinking about this change for quite a while, and had recently decided to make the move back to live with her parents. She was both afraid and unsure if she'd made the right decision, and how this would impact her future career, her family, and her ability to regain the independence she had felt while at a school in another state. I focused on Mara's aura. An aura is the energy field that surrounds us; I see it as a haze or light around the body. Usually, I do not pay attention to it unless an abnormality or change occurs in it to the point where it becomes a distraction for me. I can spend time on working specifically with someone's energy field if that is what the client is asking for during a session.

Mara had made an appointment for an intuitive reading, not energy work, but I was both feeling and seeing that her energy field was so distorted and scattered that I needed to assess what was happening in her life. It looked very much like a shattered mirror, with cracked lines running in all directions, making the reflection look very disjointed and broken. Aside from the appearance of her energy field, her energy was leaving her and bouncing all over my office. This happens when we are in a life situation where we are not able to hold our energy, and it leaves our aura field, making us feel depleted or deflated. Something or someone was pulling on her energy, and I sensed it was related to her decision to move back to Minnesota, and perhaps the stress of making a big change like this. Before I knew for sure if this was indeed the cause of her energy looking so erratic, I wanted to find out for certain its source, and then do any repair to her aura. Without understanding the source, the repaired energy field would continue to have problems. This would be like putting air in a tire that was already punctured. It would continue to leak air until the puncture was found and sealed. In Mara's case, I was seeing major cracks and rivers of her energy leaving. These were not simple leaks that over time had left her feeling deflated; these were large energy leakages that were making her feel unfocused, unsure, afraid, and unstable, as well as physically exhausted.

Since I work extensively with rocks and the energy properties of them to help in healing aura and energy fields, I immediately noticed that a huge piece of lapis on my bookshelf began to vibrate when Mara entered my office. My rocks tell me something about a client's energy field or aura. The lapis is a beautiful deep-blue stone, and its energy assists in the throat chakra, the energy center in our body that is our voice—or our control of speaking outwardly to the world. The fact that this large stone was vibrating indicated that the client needed to speak out about something in her life, but she was withholding this information. I explained how I work with the energy within all the stones and rocks I have in my office, and handed Mara the large blue lapis stone.

I began to deliver information that I was hearing from the angels and guides, and each time it was to reassure her that it was the right decision, and to stop worrying about what was left behind. I then immediately saw a gray cloud over her throat, and I felt phlegm in mine, to the point where I needed to stop, clear my throat, and take a drink of water. This was past-life energy as well as this-life energy, and there was deep fear and emotion around whatever was the cause. Again, I began to share insight from the angels as they moved in to assist in clearing the energy. They also told Mara that she was done with feeling the pain or fear around this situation. She was safe in this lifetime, and events that had happened in her past would not happen again.

Asking for assistance, I saw Mara's grandmother quickly move beside her. She acknowledged that Mara would not remember her; there had been some distance between them either in the way of physical distance or in age, as Mara was very young, if not an infant, when this grandmother crossed over. I asked Mara if her grandmother had passed, and as Mara nodded yes, she also had a very perplexed look, and said she had not known this grandmother. I continued, and explained that even though she might not remember or never knew her grandmother, she was around her, and knew Mara very well. Mara was confused by this, why a grandmother she had never known would take that role in her life. She had sensed a presence with her since she was a small child, but just thought it was an angel.

I explained to Mara that our relatives or ancestors know us, are with us, and watch over us. This was why Mara's grandmother was watching over her. Mara's grandmother was speaking to me about what had happened in the girl's life. It was she that had been gently nudging Mara to move home to Minnesota, when all others in her circle of family and friends were trying to convince her to stay where she was, and to finish her education at this out-of-state college. But her family and friends did not have the total view or the full picture of what had happened or was to happen in Mara's life. They did not understand that this move was part of her planned journey in this lifetime. She was right on track with where she needed to be.

Mara had only two years of college left, but her angels told her that somewhere during those two years she would regain her spirit and move to a location where she would live with a few friends. I paused and asked her what this meant, to regain her spirit, and if she understood this statement. She said yes. Then her grandmother spoke to me in words that were similar to what Mara was saying. Something had happened at college in Mara's first year, and it was still impacting her. She was choosing to transfer schools and return home to be supported by family and friends.

Mara's family did not fully understand her need to return, to feel safe around familiar faces and places, and in a place that she could just call home.

As we continued the reading, more messages came through for Mara that helped her validate that her grandmother was with her and was helping her through her decisions and her transition back home. It was also through her grandmother's loving words, urging Mara to tell her parents the true reasons for her move back home, that the energy stuck in Mara's throat began to move aside and clear. My own throat began to feel as if it was moving back to a normal state. Even though Mara did not know this grandmother on earth, her grandmother gave her enough information and points of validation that allowed Mara to trust that she had loved ones watching over her, who were there to offer guidance and assistance in some difficult life events and decisions. Mara felt more confident in how to approach her parents, knowing all would be OK, and this would help clear away any residual throat energy that did not need to be there any longer.

Mara asked if, after she was done with college and through this transition time, her grandmother would go away, or continue to be with her to help and guide her. I turned to Mara's grandmother, and before I could think any question, I heard her respond that she would be there to help in any situation that Mara would like her to. She then reminded Mara that there were many others that were also helping and guiding her, including her angels, guides, and other loved ones that had passed before. This was another reminder that we are never alone; no matter where we are in our physical plane, our loved ones are with us on the energetic planes.

## Paulette, a Spiritual Person Herself

Sometimes the messages help us bring clarity or an unexpected gift. Such was the case with Paulette, who was well on her spiritual journey, and had attended many of my circles. She had recently won time with me at a drawing. An unexpected gift, she recalls, as she had not planned on scheduling a reading with me and did not have any particular questions or issues that she wanted to be discussed. But her angels, guides, and light beings had other plans for her. I call her winning divine purpose and divine timing, and she was now sitting in my office. As I sat with Paulette, I could feel the energy and temperature in the room rise. We were joined by many light beings and energies that had been waiting for this time with Paulette. I was considering opening the window or just waiting to see if the energy would settle a bit. Though Paulette did not have any immediate questions, she got a *lot* of information relayed to her, specifically about things that were in the works for her spiritually, if she chose the paths being shown.

For Paulette, this reading raised her awareness regarding all the possibilities for herself as a spiritual being—a time that was warm, gentle, and supportive, and led her to new awareness of paths to take. The messages that were communicated to her from her spirit guides were both confirming and enlightening about her own energetic healing gifts, and that this was an opportunity and a time frame to take action. This was why Paulette had scheduled at this particular time, and she was definitely being guided to take advantage of the opportunities coming her way. Had she not been aware, she might not have been on the alert to watch for the opportunities. Because of this awareness and the possibilities shown to her, Paulette has paid closer attention to meditations, and to the information coming to her from multiple sources and avenues. If she had not had this reading, it would have been easy for her to discount and ignore those messages. I told her that her angels would not have allowed her *not* to hear these messages. It could have been no other way, and she was meant to hear them and see the opportunities. She *was* ready.

Since this time, Paulette says she has increased her attention to meditating, and asking for clarity on the path that was indicated to her. At that time, her world of work slowed down, which provided a lovely synchronicity for her to focus on these opportunities that will assist her on her growth path. She feels this gift of time was another intentional gift from beyond that is allowing her to focus toward possibilities. Now Paulette is both aware and spends time seeing all the possibilities that are presented to her each day. She has allowed herself to just be with her thoughts. She is at a point of accepting the thoughts and watching, as she is able to sense more vibrational activity around her and increase her own energetic sensitivities. Making this facilitated connection with her angels and guides, and being open to continuing this personal connection with them, has brought her closer to and more intimate with them. She tells me that she loves feeling their loving supportiveness in a deeper way than ever before.

## Jennifer Has Physical and Emotional Pain

Over three years ago, Jennifer became a client through a mutual friend after she had told Jennifer of the experience in clearing the fog from her life, and her ability to seek direction on a clearer path. Jennifer then made an appointment to see if the angels and guides could help bring focus to the areas of her life that seemed stuck or were not moving forward as she desired. When I met Lee, I assessed that her vibration or energy level was very low, and I asked if she had a medical condition that was pulling on her energy reserves. Jennifer said that she had undergone a complete physical just ten days prior, and was diagnosed with thyroid dysfunction and a severe vitamin D deficiency. She had started treatment for both. Over the next thirty minutes, I touched on Lee's current career status and her devastating divorce, from which she was continuing to heal. I could see the space this was taking in her heart, and told her that we would work to remove that energy so new and higher vibrational light could be placed there. As we spoke of this relationship, Lee's mother came to stand behind her. I could see the rays of her love reach over and around Lee, and as they did so, Jennifer felt her loving presence and was moved to tears. Lee's mother was conveying to Jennifer not only huge quantities of love, but also that she wanted to thank Jennifer for all she had done for her mother until the end.

Jennifer had not met me before, and was surprised that I would know anything about how she had supported her mom. Her mother had died of pancreatic cancer in 2000, and Jennifer had cared for her the last eighteen months of her life. Hearing her mother's message of acknowledgment and thanks, though extremely emotional, also gave Jennifer a deep sense of peace and reassurance. She and her mother had a deep, abiding love for each other, but whether because they were so much alike or so very different, it seemed like communication and understanding between them was strained through much of their lives.

Lee's mother conveyed to me that she wanted to apologize for being so judgmental during her time on earth. Being on the other side now, she understood the bigger picture, and was aware of the details of Lee's life. Jennifer explained that her mother had a very firm belief of conduct, and expected her children to conform and ask no questions. Stepping outside her strict code of conduct would bring down her wrath on those that dared to do so. Jennifer says that it took her many years to realize that her mother was not being strict out of disapproval, but rather out of love. She wished the best for her children, including having them become the best possible people they could be, and therefore she set very high standards for herself as well as others.

Being able to convey these messages brought peace to Jennifer with validation, and reassurance of her relationship with her mother.

At a later reading with Lee, we spoke again of her extremely difficult and painful divorce. This was at a time in her life when she already was challenged by other traumatic and emotional stress. In that marriage, Jennifer explained, she had given sixteen years to a man that she was certain she was destined to be married to for the remainder of her life. She had cared for him through three occurrences of cancer, as well as dedicatedly making every effort to positively influence his troubled teenage son. She was struggling with letting go of the disappointment, pain, or love she felt. Eleven years later, she remained stuck in that same rut, unable to move forward and distance herself from the devastation and heartbreak.

I could see that in Lee's head, she was ready to move forward. She wanted someone to enter her life so she could experience the rest of it in a loving, supporting relationship. I could also see that her heart was heavily covered with cords from her marriage. Energy cords are negative energy from other people that is attached to us. The cords pull our energy and keep us tethered to people from whom we want release. In Lee's case, I could see these cords, almost like cobwebs over her heart. They were various shades of gray, from dusty gray-white all the way to black. Each cord represented the turmoil or connection to that relationship. Some were good, but most looked gray, and the black cords represented the unhealthy attachments. Each one was pulling healthy energy from Jennifer in order to sustain its attachment. This was physically pulling on Lee's energy.

I showed Jennifer how to wipe those cords from her heart by visualizing she was reaching into her open heart and scooping out the gray and black cords. I worked with the healing angels and guides to ask for assistance in helping to disconnect these cords that were keeping her heart so painfully tied to the past. When Jennifer stood to leave, her energy field looked much clearer, and she said she felt much better. I told her to continue the exercise of removing these cords every time she thought of this past relationship. A couple of weeks later she felt the emotional hold begin to diminish, and in a month, he rarely crossed her mind. When she did think of him, it was with indifference rather than with anxiety. Clearing the heart energy allowed for new and lighter energy to enter Lee's heart. She is an amazingly loving woman, and once she cleared this, she felt the urge to become more socially active and allow others into her energy space. She now is so much more at peace, and is calmer, confident, reassured, more patient, and forgiving. Jennifer has the tools to ground and center her energy. She is more conscious of controlling her breathing, and in times of stress she knows how to use energy to protect herself, and how to rid herself of negative energy.

The angels also had messages for Jennifer to be more aware of her surroundings so she would not miss signs. As she did this, she became aware that the insights she had been given during her reading began to manifest in her life. This helped her understand and gain reassurance that she is *not* alone. She understands that she has spiritual guardians that are there to help her when she asks for their presence. She also is very aware of her mother's loving presence, and the hugs that her mother continues to bestow on her.

Jennifer later experienced a rather unusual but nonetheless traumatic accident, and sustained some minor physical injuries, including a concussion. The other injuries were slowly healing, but the effects of the concussion were not subsiding, and were giving her the most discomfort. She was experiencing a constant, deep sensation of pain and pressure in her head at the point of impact. An MRI fortunately showed no fracture or blood pooling to and/or inside the skull. Her doctor said that it could take weeks or even months to heal and for the pain to subside.

Jennifer and I had an appointment and she knew she wanted to ask for some healing energy. When she arrived at my door, she looked pale and not grounded. Her energy aura looked as if it were zigzagging everywhere in her body except where it should be going. My head immediately began to throb. I had already felt that she had something physical happening in her body, as my angels and guides had asked me to pull some of the healing crystals and to be ready to use those with Jennifer while she was here. Looking at the assortment they had asked me to pull from my shelves, I knew she had to be in pain. The throbbing pain I was feeling in my head told me immediately where that pain was.

Jennifer later forwarded me an e-mail that she'd sent to her friends, sharing her experience:

*I relayed the event of the accident and started to tell her about my injuries; cracked rib, jammed thumb, bruised tailbone, bloodied nose. Before I could bring it up, she asked me what was going on "here," and put her hand to her head exactly where I was having so much pain.*

*I told her about the concussion and the pain, so she selected a crystal for me to hold while she started a guided healing meditation. I focused on what she was asking of me when suddenly I saw the most incredibly beautiful and vibrant lights moving across my closed eyelids. Within a few seconds, Laurie told me that I may start to see colored lights, and to just keep breathing steadily and stay focused. Shortly after that, I felt the sensation of pain start to evolve into more of a tingling feeling. After a moment or two, Laurie said I might start to feel a change in the pain and to stay relaxed and let the healing spirits work. She kept the energy focus on that area for a considerable period of time, telling me that spirit was pulling in some major energy, and was still working on that area, and to stay with it. After a bit more, she suggested that I visualize the energy moving slowly down and through my body, down my legs and into the ground through the bottoms of my feet.*

*As she closed the healing part of my session, she suggested that I may be a little lightheaded but it would pass; I was and it did. We proceeded into my reading and afterward, as I was preparing to leave, I realized that the pain in my head was GONE. Not dulled or minimized—IT WAS GONE. It was gone and it stayed gone. To this day, I am astounded but so, so grateful.*

I was very grateful that Jennifer told me this story, as this was one of those times that I stepped aside and the angels and healing beings took over. I do not recall much about that session, other than my head hurt, and I knew the throbbing I was feeling deep within my head was probably the same throbbing she was feeling in hers. I reminded Lee, as I do all my clients, that this energy or the healing that they experience is not me. This was not me healing Lee, but the many loving angels, light beings, and healing energy that was made available to her. I was only helping to facilitate the energy, and could sense and see where it needed to go, and where it was moving.

Lee's success in integrating this energy into her body meant we had both been able to let go of any fears or beliefs that were inhibiting this energy. This required us to trust and move out of the way, so the healing energies could come in and go where they needed to go. We allowed the angels and guides to assist, direct, and heal. In Lee's case, they assisted in removing the emotional residue from a past relationship that needed to be cleared, but they also cleared and healed her physical pain that just needed some extra help.

# Clarity Sometimes Comes Later

Sometimes the messages do not make sense until hours, or even days, later. If a message comes through me that does not make sense to clients, I will tell my clients to write it down, remember it, and it will probably make more sense at a later time. If they are meant to understand or to find meaning in the messages, the angels will make that happen. This often means that the angels will figure out a way to get that information to the person that needs it.

This sometimes happens when I do readings at a party and one person cancels, but another steps in to take the spot. The change worries the hostess—but not me. This is often the angels, their guides, or even their loved ones encouraging them, or silently nudging them along to come for a reading. They may be seeking additional clarity on the messages they are already hearing, or they may not be hearing their messages and need a bit of help to hear, interpret, and then take action on these messages or information. Sometimes people will tell me of the overwhelming feeling they have to have a reading, or they have a feeling but can't quite pinpoint what it is they are supposed to know, or what information they are supposed hear. They only know information is there for them, and they seek out a psychic or channeler to help bring clarity. They describe it as a "drive" to be sitting in front of me. These are the energies from beyond that we are not able to explain, when we have a feeling of being pushed.

Debra had had a number of readings, but this time she had a few more questions, and wanted to focus on some things. On this occasion, as she sat down in my office, I immediately noticed that she was joined by a presence. I heard the name Nada; this presence wanted to be known and called Nada, and this energy had a motherly love attached to it. I asked Debra if this was a name for her grandmother or mother, because I often sense a feeling of familiarity such as love when a mother or grandmother joins a session. Debra didn't call her grandmother or mother Nada, and didn't know the name. I paused in the reading and asked that more information be provided. I waited for it or perhaps insight about who this presence was. I asked if this presence was here for Debra, and heard a distinct *yes*. The messages were for Debra, but I was not hearing what these messages were. No further information came forth, but I continued to feel a deep sense of love and peace.

A general calmness floated through the room, and I felt the temperature rise a bit. Typically, I don't spend a tremendous amount of time attempting to understand who the energy is if there is not an immediate knowing of it, but my experience was telling me that this energy was important to Debra. I also know from experience that if the client or I do not understand, usually more information will come during the session that will provide other clues that allow the client to make the connections. I again asked if this energy was for Debra, and again heard a firm *yes*. Most energy beings want to be acknowledged, so they work hard to get the client information that will help them connect who they are, and why they are present. Usually, by the time the session is done, there is understanding of the presence. However, at times it doesn't happen until much later; hours or even days can pass before this connection or understanding of the message or presence is made.

Sometimes the client may be nervous, and needs time after the reading to reflect on it or the information. It is usually when they are more relaxed that connections are made. Sometimes after the reading, when they are sharing their experience with family or friends, the connections or memories become clearer. Often the client will then remember and understand, and will call me or e-mail me.

In some cases, it is not until a later reading that they tell me how they remembered or how the information finally came to them. They are often shocked that they did not remember, but I know that the angels and guides provide so much information during a reading that clients are often just absorbing. It can become a bit overwhelming if they are nervous or if emotions are tied to the information received. At some readings, the client expects to connect with one loved one and another comes to her, or she expects certain information and hears other unexpected information. At the end of Debra's session, we were no closer to understanding who Nada was than when we started. I again checked in with this energy that had remained close to Debra during the entire reading. I told Debra to be on alert to information that would make this energy clear. The fact that this energy remained, and was so loving, was a sign there was importance.

I have many angelic decks of cards. These are lovely decks that I use to assist with my own messages, and I usually draw a card or two each day to see what messages my angels or celestial beings have for me. These cards allow us to get simple answers from angels and guides by shuffling the deck while asking questions. I have about ten such decks, and sometimes take them to client events to show my clients how they can use these simple tools to connect with the angels. For myself, I often choose a deck to work with over a period of time. I will often pull a card either in the morning or the evening to see what messages the angels and guides have. I often ask my angels and guides to direct me to the deck they want me to use.

A few days after Debra's reading, I went to the deck of cards that I had been working with that week. I had the urge to use another deck of angel cards. As I looked at the decks I let my hands pull one from the stack. This was the Ascended Masters deck. A favorite, but not one I use for messages the angels want to give to me personally. I took the deck of cards from its box and began to slowly shuffle. As I did, I asked my angels and guides what information they wanted me to know this day, and to please provide me with this. As I was thinking this, a card dropped from the deck, as if invisible hands had simply plucked it from the deck and let it fall to the floor. I laughed and commented that I guessed it was to be my card for the day. The card had fallen face-up. As I bent to pick up the card, I could see the name on it was Mother, Wife, Sister, Daughter, but at the bottom of the card, under the picture, I noticed for the first time the name Lady Nada. I had used this deck in the past, but had never noticed the Mother, Wife, Sister, Daughter card also had an Ascended Master named Lady Nada. Wow. I burst out laughing, and spoke to the energy I was now feeling in the room, understanding I was not going to sleep until her message to me was complete.

It was late in the night, but I went down to my office and e-mailed Debra to tell her that the energy of Nada had made her presence known. I felt that Lady Nada was not going to allow me to wait until the morning to write to Debra about this experience. I felt it was important that Debra know about this energy, and how I now understood that Debra was to work with this Ascended Master. I took the card and the book detailing the meaning of the cards, and typed an e-mail to Debra explaining the card, and how I believed Nada wanted to work with her.

Below is that e-mail:

*Hi Debra – I thought I would write this, as I believe the message is for you. I was shuffling an angel deck and a card fell to the floor, , and it was Lady Nada. She represents Mother, Wife, Sister, and Daughter. She is an Ascended Master who works with Saint-Germain and Archangel Michael to help bring about balance of the male and female energies in the world. Her name signifies the beautiful sound of the void of silence, where peace is found. I believe she is with you, because of the work that you do, and the work that you will continue to do with women. Thank you for allowing this introduction to a wonderful master, and she made it known just who she is.*

Debra e-mailed me later that day:

*Wow! And thank you, dear Laurie. Every night, before I go to sleep, I pray and meditate with my Celtic devotional. Each night has a specific meditation based on the phase of the moon. Last night, the meditation was simply this line: "The silent accord of love."*

*I read it and thought to myself that I wished I weren't so tired so that I could ponder it. Instead, I shut off the light and went right to sleep around 10:00 p.m.*

*I awoke around 1:00 a.m., and had this strong urge to check my cell phone for e-mail. I tried to resist, telling myself not to do that electronic stuff in bed or I would never be able to get back to sleep.*

*Still, the pull was so persistent that I did open my e-mail and discovered your message about Lady Nada. The beautiful sound of the void of silence where peace is found.*

*Immediately, I knew that she was the presence I experienced one day as I sat in my sacred space with my eyes closed (several months ago). I heard her come and stand beside me, and it was a feeling that the presence was benevolent and pure love. That she was there/here for me, by my side.*

*Thank you so very much. I am incredibly grateful to you for taking the time to tell me. It is so affirming and touching, and I feel, deep within me, that this knowledge has changed me already. I cannot thank you enough. Blessings to you and your beautiful gift.*

*—Debra*

When I sent the e-mail to Debra, I knew that I would not be allowed to rest until the information had been sent, and the connection had been completed. It was important to Lady Nada that this communication was complete, and that Debra received this information. Had it not been important, that card wouldn't have fallen on the floor. It wasn't a choice to send the e-mail; it simply had to be done. Through my angels and guides, I have learned to follow their direction, and trust the information that they provide to me or to my clients. Sending this information was a completion or a continuation of the information they provided to me. It was not a mystery that needed to be solved; rather, it was a connection that needed to happen as a way of opening the door for both Lady Nada and Debra to begin or continue the process of working together.

## Kristin and the Little Boy

Another connection or "remembered" information happened at an intuitive party to which Kristin had invited her co-workers, and I was doing readings. Kristin's guests went first, and when they were all done, she sat down across from me to begin her reading. Immediately a little boy joined her. I asked if she had a little brother that had died as an infant. I could feel Kristin's mother on the other side move forward, and was showing me how she was rocking a baby. As a grandma now, she was happy that she was being asked to help rock the babies, and was enjoying a reconnection. Kristin replied that yes, her brother had died, but not as an infant. I told her that definitely there was an infant who was around her often, and was telling her that he was OK, and that he would see her again someday. She looked puzzled and said she was mystified, and did not know who this little energy might be—but she was happy that this little boy and his loving energy were with her.

I told Kristin that I thought his name was Eric or Eddie or some version of that, but it felt more international, so it might have been spelled or pronounced differently. We chose to focus the remainder of her time speaking with her mother and father, who were waiting patiently to speak with her. Her father had been waiting quite a while, and both parents were overlaying love on her. Kristin asked both parents questions, and her father told her she was on track with a project she was pursuing. I did not know what this meant, but when I asked Kristin if she understood this message or if she needed more information, she was clear. It was related to some research she had started, but was not sure if she should continue to pursue it. It had been one of the questions on which she had wanted guidance from her father, and he had given her the acknowledgment of her work, and that yes, she was to continue to pursue it. He was very proud of her, and acknowledged that this research was not easy.

The next time I saw Kristin, she said that shortly after her reading, she had gone out to dinner with her family and told them about her experience. She also related the story about the baby-boy energy that came through, and she did not know who he was. Her daughter immediately knew who the little-boy energy was, and reminded Kristin of a miscarriage. Though she never knew the sex of the child, this energy was her little boy. She was overjoyed to learn that he was OK, and even more overjoyed that she would see him again someday. The name Eric or Eddie was probably more like Erikki which made sense to her also, given her ancestry and heritage. Erikki is Finnish for Eric.

Often I do not get to hear when a client makes the connection and understands the messages, so when it does happen, I know that the angels and guides were continuing to work their magic in assisting with this work. I was very grateful to Kristin for telling me.

## Little Girl in a Pretty Dress

Sometimes even I do not make the connections until a later time. In this case, I was at an intuitive party made up of members from one family. I was not told who was related to whom, and I usually prefer not to know because the energetic beings or loved ones come in as needed. At this party, I did a reading for a young mother whose girl child had died in infancy of an illness. As the reading began, I immediately saw a beautiful child about the age of two standing in a sunny field. She was holding the bottom of her dress with both hands. She was shifting the dress back and forth, clearly wanting me to see that she very happy with this dress.

In the reading, I was now seeing her as slightly older. This was her method of telling her mom that she was growing up, and was experiencing the joys of learning to walk and run in the sunshine. She was a very happy and beautiful child. She clearly wanted her mom to know that she was better, and the illness had left her after she passed. She continued to show me her dress. I felt a grandmother's presence, and the mother said that this would be her daughter's great-grandmother. The great-grandmother shared that though she loved rocking the babies in heaven, this little girl would have nothing to do with rocking when there was so much to explore. She would, however, spend time with the great-grandmother when she was tired or just wanted some hugs. The mother laughed, saying that this would be like her other very-active children who never wanted to sit on their grandmother's lap.

We concluded the reading, and as I prepared for the next client, the little girl lingered with me. I told her that she needed to leave, and I distinctly heard her say, "No, I don't want to." I chuckled, thinking that they do keep many of the same traits after they cross over that they had here on earth; of course, why would they be any different? When the next client walked into the room, the little girl remained. As I spoke to this woman, I could feel her mother's energy. Her mother had crossed over when she was very young, and she had missed her dearly over the years. She wanted to know that her mother was OK, and was with the family. She also asked if she saw all the babies. Her mother began to show me how she would rock the babies, and I knew this was rocking babies that had crossed over. They were being cared for and loved by this grandmother.

The little girl in the dress joined us again. She was now sitting on the grandmother's lap, but this was not her grandmother—her grandmother was sitting on the couch in front of me. The little girl was sitting on her great-grandmother's lap. I now made the connection. Quickly, she was off her lap and again showing me the dress. She would spin around so it would flare out, and would then hold the bottom and move it back and forth. I sensed that she liked the feel of this very special dress. When I asked the grandmother with me the significance of this dress, she began to cry. She had brought a special dress for the little girl to wear for her funeral. Dying very young, she had not enjoyed frilly dresses, so the grandmother wanted her to have a pretty dress.

# Chapter 10

# Pain Is Felt Only Here—Not There

Most people want to know that our loved ones are no longer in pain. This would include any physical or emotional pain that they may have felt while here on earth. The pain is only felt here. We do not carry this pain to the other side. When we leave this earthly plane and go to the spirit world, we have peace, joy, and love.

When we die, we attend the review of our life before the council of elders. Anything we have not completed and all those items we agreed to accomplish are reviewed. We go through a healing process, and some would like to call it a hospital-like environment that assists us in healing any of our earthly physical or emotional pain. Some people like to have that visual. I see individuals with loved ones, angels, guides, and masters—all there to meet them. They are surrounded by love, joy, and a great amount of peace. All are welcomed with loving open arms. I do not believe that anyone goes to a place called hell. I do know that everyone goes through this healing process. How much "work" they must do determines the number of resources there to assist them, and the amount of time required.

For some, I have seen this time go very quickly; for others, it takes a long time. It depends on the individual souls, what they accomplished on earth in comparison to their goals, and how they died.

I consistently hear from all those that have crossed over that they are fine. This is the number-one message they want us to hear. This may often sound like a fake or staged response, and many skeptical people have said that is just telling a loved one what he/she wants to hear. Yes, it's true, but it is equally important that we hear and understand this message. It is no different from taking a long flight and, when we land, calling to let our loved ones know that we have arrived. It is a familiar connection with our loved ones, so why would this connection stop once we have crossed over?

## Freeing Grandma's Spirit

Recently I did a small party for a group of women. As I began a reading for one of the last women, I saw an elderly woman come stand alongside her. She appeared very stiff and rigid in her movements. I could feel the elderly woman's love that she was raining down on the younger woman, but she continued to remain stationary, and didn't say anything. She was waiting for something. I continued with the reading, waiting for either the elderly woman to say something or the angels to let me know when or if I should ask about this elderly woman. She seemed to very purposely say nothing. She was waiting for acknowledgment from the younger woman. Toward the end of the reading, the young woman asked about her new husband's grandmother. Though she had never met this woman, she wondered if she was there, and if the grandmother liked her. This was the rigid woman standing beside this younger woman's chair. When I acknowledged the grandmother, it was like her joints suddenly unlocked, and I could see her energy flutter off in the distance, gaining movement as she went. I felt such extreme joy that it brought tears to my eyes.

I told the group that with this younger woman asking about the grandmother she had not known, she had somehow assisted in expediting her healing. I asked the elderly woman to return to us and explain what had happened. I could see her energy dancing, and I continued to feel the love and joy she felt toward this younger woman. The elderly woman told me that she had a long, painful death. I was not able to pinpoint the illness that took away her mobility. I told the young woman that it felt muscular or that her muscles could not move. The young woman validated that yes, the grandmother had suffered long and finally died of a muscular disease. The elderly woman wanted to make sure this young woman understood that the rigidness was gone and she was able to move about freely. Her dancing and fluttering around like a butterfly was very symbolic of her ability to move freely and no longer be locked in the rigidness of her body.

I felt very blessed to have witnessed this, and explained to the group that they had been a part of the realization of the elderly woman that she had regained her freedom of movement. She was no longer locked into that rigidness that she had carried here on earth. This was a very important message for the young woman to carry back to her husband and his family, and validated that the grandmother had been healed as she crossed over and had regained her love of movement. She specifically wanted to show the younger woman that she was fine and was moving, and that included dancing because she was pain-free.

Those who have passed are not experiencing the same reference points or beliefs that we have here on earth. Many clients worry unnecessary about little events or misunderstandings that happened with their loved one. They hold on to the worry that their loved one will remember *that* little item as the event that defines how they felt about them while they were here. When we die and cross over, and we stand before the review board, we review our lives and events and how we handled them. But then they are done, and any emotion or harsh feelings that may have been there—is replaced with love. There is *only* love. Sometimes they communicate events or a memory only as a means for the client to be able to validate that it is them. More importantly, it can be to release the feelings still held by the client. There is only love, and they want any lower vibrational energy such as anger, guilt, sadness, jealousy, or hopelessness replaced by the feeling of love. They cover us with love to assist us in letting go of an emotion that is only here—not there.

Sometimes they provide advice for us to let a situation alone, allowing it to work itself through without intervention. Such was the case with sisters that came to me to speak to their mother who had died. Her mother was very clear that all had been done, and nothing more medically could have helped her. In her words, it was time for her to go. The two daughters understood this, and felt that everything had been done, but their older sister did not agree, and felt more treatments could have been tried. As a result, she had refrained from speaking to family members. The two sisters and a brother had tried without success, even telling her that their mother would not want her shunning the family. The family was in turmoil over what to do, and who should try to do it. Their mother provided calming words from beyond, telling them to leave it be, allowing the sibling to have time to heal. No one had to do anything but let her know they loved her, and when she was ready they would all come back together.

These words of validation to the sisters told them that their mother did not expect them to take action. They worried that they were letting her down if they did nothing, and were struggling with what actions she would want them to take. They gained clarity, and with their mother's message gained great peace.

During Jordan's reading I once again noticed her father dancing behind her. Today I was having difficulty determining if it was a waltz or simply freestyle dancing. The first time I'd met Jordan, her father, had spent the entire reading dancing behind her. Jordan shared with me that his family told stories of times when they would catch him ballroom dancing in the kitchen. He loved to dance, though he was not a trained ballroom dancer. During all Jordan's reading he would not *stop* dancing, so we asked him: why the continual movement? This question was simply followed by a very straightforward message that since he loved to dance, and had been in so much pain prior to his passing, he was choosing this action to remind his family, and anyone that could see him, that he was perfectly fine and enjoying his freedom of movement.

# Chapter 11

# Exiting Early

This chapter was the most difficult one to write. Not because the material and content were not there, but due to my own fear of what I would learn in the process of writing. It was my own fear of not getting it right, my inability to turn off my own filters. It was my fear of being judged about what I should or should not include.

As I was writing the original outline for this book, I added the chapter related to suicide, but later pulled it out. When I actually started to write the book, messages would come through to some of my clients regarding early death, and I was urged to write the chapter. I tried putting this chapter in the middle of the book, then at the very end of the book, and then pulled it out again. This went on for a while as my ego battled with the angels and angelic beings from other dimensions. Whether or not the chapter should be included was an ongoing question. As I began to write more, each chapter came together simply, very well-orchestrated, and with ease and grace. I would tell my friends that it was like angels and loved ones were standing behind me, wanting to be involved in this project. The truth was that many loved ones and angels stood behind me when I would write.

Once again, when I got to the chapter on suicide, I wrote around it, leaving the heading in place and the pages between empty, waiting for material and information to be added. I looked at the heading and its blank pages on the computer screen. I committed to writing about this topic, and asked again for assistance from my loved ones, and other loved ones that wanted us to hear. Early death, suicide, exiting early—I could hear my cousin's faint voice asking me to share, to listen, to learn, and to teach about exiting early. All the messages and information were available to me, but would I be brave enough? Would I be worthy enough to understand and then be able to put the words on paper? And I heard one simple word: *trust*. It was not easy to trust, but I had to focus on it. I admitted to myself that I was avoiding writing this chapter. As I began to peel away the layers of fear, and to believe all that I needed to hear would be brought to me, the help came, but in the form of clients.

My calendar is usually the busiest in December and January, with large parties and events, but this particular year my calendar looked very different. In December it was completely filled, but January was nearly empty. I interpreted this as getting a cosmic break in my schedule. Wow, was I wrong.

I had a rest period of a few days, and then my phone began to ring, but these requests were for private readings—not parties or events. My first clients in the week were two younger women. At the end of their readings, Marissa asked about her uncle because the family wanted to know if he was OK. I heard the message from him that he had committed suicide, and her question was really if he had made it to heaven. Yes, he was in heaven.

In the next few days, four more clients each had someone in their life that had exited early. Later in that same week I met Carolyn. When I met her and her friend at the door, I asked if they had had any difficulty finding my office, and immediately heard a voice tell me that he was with them in the car as they were "over there," in the general area of a large shopping mall. Whoever was speaking to me from beyond was laughing at the fact that the women had gotten lost, and had been circling the neighborhood for quite some time. I showed them both into my office and asked who wanted to be first, but I was stopped by a voice that directed me to Carolyn, the woman to my left. I told her that she had a male standing next to her, and he wanted her to be first. He had been with them while they were lost, and was still laughing at their experience in getting to my home. As I told her, both women laughed. They had gotten lost and had stopped at the shopping mall parking lot to get directions. In talking about who would go first, Carolyn had said she was nervous and a bit scared, so she wanted her friend to go first. Carolyn had never had a reading before, and her friend had, so they decided that Carolyn would have hers second. However, someone else had already decided that her reading was going to be first. This was Carolyn's father, and he had been waiting to connect with her. I told Carolyn and her friend that my office had gotten so hot that I had to open the window. As it turned out, I left my office window open the entire time of the reading, and this was January in Minnesota.

Carolyn had been fourteen when her father died. His death had been a shock for her and the entire family. He had exited early at his own hand, having committed suicide. Carolyn, her sisters, and her mother had not been prepared for this, and as in all deaths, the pain had gone deep. Carolyn had not been sure that she wanted answers to her questions, but now, sitting across from me, her father was providing her with answers. Above all else, he was telling her how much he loved her, and that he was sorry for leaving her, her sisters, and her mother as he did many, many, many years ago. He was sorry for the pain, for what he had missed in her life; sorry that he had caused such deep hurt. He was not ashamed, nor was he guilty, but he was in deep pain. I could feel the stabbing in my own heart as I briefly experienced how deep his pain ran. His love for his family ran as deep as his pain. He had grown and learned from his experience. We finished Carolyn's reading, and I then I began the reading for her friend Carolyn's father remained standing to her left immersing her in love. When I was nearly done with the reading for Carolyn's friend, we both felt her father leave. I looked at Carolyn and she asked, "He is gone, isn't he?" I responded, "Yes, but he is never far from you, and now you know that blanket of warmth you felt is him showering you with love." Carolyn gasped, "I could feel him!"

Before they left, I hugged them both. During a small break between them and the next two clients, I sat quietly in my office. I meditated and asked that the love from her father continue to flow over Carolyn, and that the angels assist in any way they felt was needed.

My next clients arrived, and wanted their readings together. I showed them into my office and began the reading with Amy. At the end of the reading, she asked if I could see her uncle. He, too, had committed suicide. I began to see the now familiar images in my mind's eye; this was the sixth loved one that week that had exited early. I instantly knew that they were all trying not only to get their loved one's attention, but to reach out to me and assist in getting their messages out and beyond. And so this chapter came to be, with the help of those loved ones that were so insistent in sharing their story.

After I finished with my last clients, I thanked my guides and angels, and was about to shut down my computer and turn in for the night. Sitting at my computer, I was being urged to handle just a few more e-mails before turning everything off. One of those e-mails was to Carolyn, to tell her about this book I was writing, and ask if I could talk further with her and her father as a way to share their messages. I knew Carolyn would agree. I knew this because I also knew her father had been behind all those arrangements for these particular clients. He was bold in life, and he was showing his boldness in the afterlife by organizing. Never in all my years of doing private readings or parties have I had so many early exits as in that week. There were definitely some powerful messages there, and definitely some energies were involved in coordinating all these people in the same week. When I wrote Carolyn, I believe her dad was standing behind me. She replied to my e-mail the next day, and we met a few days later.

As Carolyn and I settled in to begin talking, I explained that she was the fifth person in a week that had come to see me, each having someone very close that had exited early. I explained how when I was younger I lost two cousins to suicide, and it was my younger cousin that had first suggested I write about this topic. I spoke with my father about this, but neither felt comfortable approaching my uncle. I had left it to the angels, guides, and other loved ones to bring forward what was needed, and I simply trusted that they would do so.

Carolyn then told me that over a year ago a co-worker had given her my business card, and she had thought of calling for an appointment, but was afraid. It was a few weeks ago that she had felt an overwhelming urge to contact me. She was not able to find my business card, but knew that her co-worker had texted the information. She admitted that she had to go back through all her text messages to find the one that had my contact information. We laughed at the well-orchestrated events. When clients call for an appointment, they typically have to wait such a long time, as I usually get booked well in advance; however, that week I was able to accommodate all the clients that needed to be there.

I told Carolyn that the number-one question people ask is if their loved one is all right. I do not know that we will ever fully understand everything about life and death, and we will never be able to fully experience death until we die, but messages and information need to be shared about both. Why would dying from suicide be any different? When people die, no matter how they die, it impacts all their loved ones. Death is painful for those left behind, and when a loved one exits earlier than expected, it is a shock. We are unprepared, surprised, and as humans we typically do not like to be unprepared for anything. Most of us live our entire lives as problem solvers, fixers, and planners, in all those activities we feel we can control. In death, we have no control and no planning. It happens, and we do not like the fact that we were not able to stop, change, or prevent death.

What shocks us about suicide is that it is at that person's own hands. It is difficult to understand murder, or when someone kills another person, but when a loved one departs at his/her own hand, it leaves the family members struggling to understand why. Some of those left behind sink deep into guilt, anger, and other lower-energy emotions that leave us doubting if we understood our loved one. Sometimes we become suspicious about the suicide simply because we cannot fathom that our loved one would do that. This is very common, as with Carolyn. Although the police ruled it a suicide because letters were left for the family members, the family had a hard time believing he would do this. We may begin to doubt ourselves, sensing that life can be pulled away too quickly, and without warning. Suicide can leave tattered emotions and unanswered questions. It often has long-term effects for those left behind. The bottom line is that it is painful. I could clearly hear Carolyn's father's words: there simply is no way to put all those feelings into words that others could feel, unless they had experienced it themselves. There simply is no other way to write about these feelings other than that it shocks us to our core, and leaves us with no solutions, nothing to fix, nothing to change or redo. It is final and complete, and it leaves an empty feeling in our core, our soul. It is as if someone has drilled holes in our hearts, and in our soul, and what is left behind are the holes that can never be refilled or replaced in this lifetime.

If I can help anyone make a connection with someone that he/she has lost in this lifetime, and it assists in the healing process, then I have used my gift as it was meant to be used. If I am able to connect someone with a loved one that shares healing messages, then I have used my gift as it is meant to be used. If I am able to explain these messages to a greater audience to help them understand, then I have used my gifts as they are meant to be used. If those that have crossed over assist in any of these healing processes, they are assisting their loved ones and themselves in the healing process, and we all benefit from that.

If at the end of our conversation with her dad, Carolyn did not want to include any of it in this book, that would be fine, but as those words left my mouth, I knew some very important messages needed to be communicated. And so we began the conversation with Carolyn's father, William Martin Opsahl Jr., who preferred to be called Butch.

At the top of Butch's list was that he wanted us to know that people who commit suicide do go to heaven. When they leave this earth and move toward the light, they are surrounded by immense love and loving beings. They are not punished and sent to a dark place to live in isolation; they are sent to the light where they are embraced. They have just left the pain of being in a third-dimension body, which is dense and heavy in energetic weight, and are then thrust outward into lightness or weightlessness.

Carolyn's dad showed me the image of a balloon shooting upward into the sky—free, light, and floating. He described all his earthly pain falling away, and seeing the beauty of everything all around him. Leading up to the time that Butch exited, he had become overwhelmed by financial decisions he had made, and by friendships and relationships that hurt his family. He loved to live boldly and be the center of attention, but in doing so, he admitted to making irresponsible decisions for himself and his family. He had betrayed those he loved the most. He left at a time in his life when the emotional stress outweighed his drive to see another solution. At that point, he saw no other solution. A proud man who typically felt he could fix everything, without the help of others, he was not able to fix this. He was embarrassed; he had already sought financial help from others and felt he could not ask again. He was done—and had decided.

Carolyn asked me if it had been him that had called. I heard him say very faintly that he just wanted to hear a voice. First, he had sat quietly in his car outside his office, finding the strength to move forward with his actions; then in his office quite a while, thinking. He made a few phone calls, one to his home. Had anyone picked up the phone, it would not have mattered. Again I heard him faintly say, "It was all right that no one answered because the decision had already been made."

Carolyn said on that evening their mom was at work, and she was home with her sister. The phone rang, and as most teens do, they began to argue about who should answer it. By the time they had decided, it had stopped ringing. This was a healing moment for Carolyn, as I believe it had weighed heavily on her and her sister's minds all these years. Her dad was glad they had not picked up the phone because they would possibly have held the guilt of talking to him and not stopping him. The fact was, Butch had made his decision, and he was committed to carrying it out because he didn't see any other way. Through all the emotional pain that he had been feeling, as he exited his body and this dimension, he described the beauty he began to see and feel—the freedom from all that he left behind.

Carolyn asked if he had been with them the days after he left. He said that he had tried to get the attention of everyone while they attended the funeral and were in his house, to let them know he was still there, but no one could hear him. I could see him walking up to family members and attempting over and over to get them to look at him, talk to him, or notice him. As much as he felt the freedom from his earthly body and the stresses he had carried on earth, he also felt the immense sorrow of seeing his family in such pain, and the frustration of not being able to have them see him. He wanted to explain.

Carolyn told me that he had written letters to all of them, and as they huddled together reading them, they asked their mother if he had gone to heaven. They all agreed that he had. We all want to believe our loved ones go to heaven. Carolyn's dad was telling her that he went to heaven, and he was greeted with love. His pain came when he was taken in front of the board of elders and required to review his life. He reviewed his early childhood and all the events leading up to his death. He lingered on some, and as I sat with Carolyn, I felt he was being allowed to replay some of those events. He was lingering on the happier events, and was not being asked to look at other events again, as it would create pain. He had already done that during the initial review. He stayed on the early years and the happy moments with his kids. He wanted Carolyn to know that she was deeply loved.

I felt him stop at the midpoint between what he had experienced and lived on earth, and what would have been and the events he would have experienced had he lived onward. "Life interrupted" meant he had impacted his soul family, and the plan that had been so well planned and orchestrated for all. The magnitude of the impact on others was the pain he had felt so deeply, and he was not able to put this into words at all—other than it was more painful than the depression and the events that had led up to his death, more painful than the actual death and the fear he experienced right before he shot himself. This pain was the realization of all that he would miss in this lifetime. There was no going back. He told me he had always been able to fix it, make it better, or figure out a plan B. In this case there was nothing. He was powerless, and the realization of the finality was overwhelming. I was sensing a much different energy than the way he lived, and Carolyn's father was showing me how much he had learned and shifted since he died. He had been doing quite a bit of work to heal and learn, and though he was not done with all that he needed to learn, he admitted he was in a much better place. His apology was filled with deep love for all those he thought he'd hurt, and he was sorry for all that he had missed by leaving early.

When I asked Butch if this was in his journey plan—meaning, was his suicide part of an overall plan, or did he indeed leave early—he confirmed that it was not part of the plan, and that he had decided to leave this life earlier than what was planned. Other times in his life he had thought of suicide, but had worked through those thoughts and emotions. He said this time it was different, and he had felt there was no way.

I felt Butch's energy level decrease. I explained to Carolyn that for him to spend this much time communicating to us was an extreme energy drain on him. He must move into a lower vibration, and this gets very tiresome. I then had to raise my own energy level, and I asked for the angels and other loved ones to provide an energy boost to help us. The angels came and began to assist both of us, and I felt such deep gratitude for all that were helping to make this information available. It was healing for Carolyn and her father, and the messages will also help others who read this book. Carolyn's father wanted her to know that he loved her and was fine. This is a consistent message that many who cross over want to send their loved ones. Although he had left his family earlier than expected, he did not love them any less, and his journey with them continued, only it was from a distance. He still feels the love from his family.

On this night, as his energy began to waver from all the work he was doing, he thanked her for being brave, bold, and curious. In those regards, Carolyn is much like her father. It took courage and deep love to make that first appointment with me. Her courage continued as we sat for over two hours talking with her father and about him and her family. During this time, he consistently was enveloping her with love and messages that he continues to love her and her family very deeply, with a last reminder that the journey does not end; it continues on and on and on.

Since then, I have done other readings with Butch's family members, and he makes his presence boldly known. I am grateful for the introduction to him and his family, and their trust in the process, as well as the teachings that he has provided for all reading this book. He also assisted in bringing some healing closure and new beginnings to his family. Even now, he continues to acknowledge the gift of life and the gift of life after death. Both continue forward and with experience on both dimensions. We often think that healing only happens for those here on earth, but clearly, it was through his loving teaching that the lessons of life and the lessons of beyond continue, just as does the healing of our hearts.

# Chapter 12

# A Sister's Love

Sandy and I met while I was doing an intuitive party a number of years ago. When I was first introduced to her, I was so distracted by the very large, inter-dimensional, alien-looking guide standing behind her that I stumbled on my words. He was tied to other universes, and I felt very honored to be in his presence. This was Sandy's first reading, and I quickly needed to balance how I would begin to describe what I was seeing and feeling without sending her home with nightmares. Her guide was large and different-looking, but he was and remains a very loving energy in her life, and very powerful in directing her on this journey. He was excited to have her know him. Sandy remembers that time, and because I was not able to pronounce his name, he laughed and told her she could call him anything, which left the door wide open for her to have some fun with it. His humor definitely matches hers.

Sandy, being a very well-organized leader, took copious notes. When I began this book, she graciously offered her notes. We met recently to review them and once again talk to her brother, Jim. In that first reading Sandy had been able to connect with her brother on a different level. For both, it moved them light-years along the path of healing.

At first, Jim was crouched down, almost in a fetal position. He would not look at me. He was filled with such deep remorse that I had a difficult time sensing any other words or emotions. He was deeply saddened by the life he had led, and wanted to say he was sorry for all the things he had done in his lifetime. He hadn't had an opportunity to say all that he wanted to before he had passed, but now he held back. He was embarrassed, and concerned that he would not be heard. I asked the angels to assist, and began to share some of his words with Sandy. She listened and asked some questions, but took all his messages to heart. I realized the angels were assisting her during this time, and they were also lovingly providing Jim guidance, and time to get his message to Sandy. She had never been to an intuitive, psychic, or channeler, and had no idea what to expect. When she was invited to this event, she trusted and said an unwavering yes. I believe her brother had his hand in getting her to that event; he needed to talk to her. How lovely to see the mending of hearts between a brother and sister.

Sandy is a very dynamic woman educated in the medical field. She is also a healer in this lifetime, working in a large hospital organization in the Minneapolis area. With her background in health-care services, she understands the importance in the healing process when family and friends are involved. She understands the impact of illness and other health-related issues. She describes herself as living her whole life with an older brother who had suffered from mental health issues. This impacted not only her, but her entire family. Sandy writes:

> *I always felt like we had a "black cloud" over us. My brother spent his lifetime in prison and that was his home and his family. He was a strong leader within the safety of those walls. My mom and I visited him the week before he died, which was very healing. But the TRUE healing came from my first reading with you. Oppression lifted, bridges mended, built and healed.*

In that first reading, as we continued to listen to Jim's words, he poured down love on Sandy and asked her to share these messages with his mom. He wanted her to know that when he passed, it was his time. He could not change, and so it was time for him to pass. He said it was important for his mom to know that he loved her and heard his apology.

While he was being heard, I could feel the love and the energy around it move back and forth between Sandy and Jim as he began to stand in the full lightness. He felt that she understood him. He stood to face me, and then to acknowledge his sister. He thanked both of us because this clearly was a healing moment for them.

The last weekend Sandy visited Jim was a gift on many levels. Jim was too sick to be in his prison cell, so that last visit was in his hospital room. Sandy's background in the medical field made the environment very familiar, and allowed Jim to be comfortable.

Sandy told me Jim loved the Beatles, and his family would tease him that he would have been the fifth Beatle if he could have. Sandy's understanding of the use of music in healing made her wish she had brought some Beatles music to his hospital room when he was so sick. Sandy and her mom left him on Monday, and he died on Wednesday. Jim told Sandy that he was grateful for the illness. Not at the time he was experiencing it, but he now fully understood his purpose for being there in that hospital room that last weekend. He had become so sick that he could never stay warm, and needed special permission to receive an extra blanket for medical purposes. He knew Sandy felt bad about that. He said that he was deeply grateful that his mom and sister saw him at the hospital. After decades of no communication, they had made the cross-country trip to see him because he was so sick. Jim again apologized for all that he had done, and all the pain he had caused in so many lives. He was sorry he had led such a separate life from the rest of his family. The pain around his life was lifting.

The second time I did a reading for Sandy, she checked in with her brother. His energy was now different; very light, happy. He had been to visit her and her family, sending them love any chance he could. Sandy asked him what he was doing now, and he responded, "Today I am riding a motorcycle, havin' fun. There are no rules in heaven."

Sandy and I met to discuss Jim's story—more likely, Jim arranged for us to meet so we would collaborate to tell his story—and as we did so, he smiled down on both of us. She again told me the motorcycle comment was her favorite. The symbolism in it was that in this life he hated rules, laws, and anything that felt controlling. He was free. Sandy also showed me a memoir their mother put together after his death. This hardcover photo and memory book was then given to loved ones. Jim was an artist, and one of his most amazing drawings was that of a motorcycle, clearly showing his love for it.

When Sandy and I talked about her previous sessions, she told how healing all the messages were for her and her family. The received messages and those shown his mannerisms were things that only they would know, and these were important to allow the healing to happen, and close the gap left by decades of time.

In this session, Jim was now acting as big brother for Sandy. He had loving words for her, but also wanted her to hear this: "Life is short, do not wait." This was a perfect message for her at that point in her life. He was behind her, supporting her. He also wanted to thank her for being brave during that first session so the connection could happen, and the healing could begin. He called her his earth angel because during her first reading, and that first connection with him, her initial action was that of simply listening and not judging. That simple act of listening and loving allowed him to move from a crouched position in darkness to an upright position in the light. Love truly does heal all.

We asked Jim what he wanted us to know, and he had these messages. The journey continues, it does not stop, and it is always the adventure that we see it to be. The healing continues. This had caught him by surprise, but it follows the theory that the journey continues, so love, healing, and all else would also continue. Love continues and is forever, and though there is distance between earth and heaven, with time, love continues to grow, shifting and expanding. It is never gone, it is forever available, and it continues forever. Lastly, it just is. It is all so perfectly orchestrated, and we need to believe in that. Sandy marveled at the events that led her to have a reading with me. We laughed and acknowledged the number of hands that must have assisted in having that happen, as it was all perfectly aligned.

Sandy asked if Jim was the one that I saw next to her, laughing. I sensed that he has a great sense of humor, and perhaps his family did not get to see this lightness and happiness in him while he was here. He told me he is at peace, and is happy. The word *peace* was important, and I began to see some sort of image that looked like an upside-down Y as Jim was telling me he is at peace.

As I talked about the importance of *peace*, Sandy pulled a copy of a drawing from things she'd brought with her that evening. It was from a card Sandy had purchased for Jim a month before he died. The main word on the card was *peace*—but she had shaded the peace symbol around the word peace. This was the upside-down Y that I had been seeing or the peace symbol that became very popular in the 1960s.

As I looked through Jim's memory book, I was now looking at the man I had only known as an energetic feeling. He was an artist that had the ability to draw amazing pictures with meticulous detail; he loved music, especially the Beatles. Sandy said earlier that he had one CD by Sarah McLachlan, and that Jim would sleep during the day and listen to this CD at night so he could do it in quiet, without interruptions. As she was telling this story, Jim asked if she knew the song, "Do you remember me?" Sandy was not familiar with that song.

A few days later Sandy e-mailed me this note.

> *I bought a new CD last night—you guessed it! I consider it "a date with my brother."*
>
> *Smile. Sandy*

The healing continues in the words of Sarah McLachlan's song.

I will remember you, will you remember me?

Don't let your life pass you by...

## More Pieces Come Together

Later that same year, I was driven by a force I could not explain to take my two children to see the King Tut exhibit at the Minnesota Science Museum. It was a busy summer, and we were having a difficult time finding a weekend where we would not be rushed and could enjoy our time viewing the exhibit. We needed to pre-purchase tickets with assigned times due to the overwhelming attendance. The urge to go to this exhibit was energetically charged, and I knew there had to be a greater purpose for my sense of urgency to take the kids, but aligning times was tough. That very next weekend I had an event cancellation, and I checked for availability of tickets. We laughed at how simply everything seemed to come together for us that afternoon.

Even before going into the exhibit area at the Science Museum, my children and I could already feel the energy of relics of Tut. We moved slowly with the crowd, yet felt driven by an energy to get to somewhere ahead of us. Something was pulling us. Many pieces held the vibration of that time.

As I turned a corner, before me was a large statue of Tut's royal guard. I let out a huge sigh, which I thought was a quiet one, but apparently it was loud enough to get the attention of people both ahead of and behind me in the exhibit line. This guard looked somewhat like Sandy's big alien-like guide; however, he was not so alien-like anymore. I felt acknowledgment, and a huge energy rushed over me. We sat in this energy for a short while, until crowds began to push in on the pristine energy. It was time to go. We stopped for dinner on the drive home, and none of us could stop talking about the energy we experienced—not how the exhibit looked, but how we felt in its different rooms. How lucky we were to have been drawn to that exhibit, and to experience its energy and see an energy in statue form. Later that evening after I got home, I wrote Sandy an e-mail telling her that I'd met the energy I'd seen when I first met her. Her very large inter-dimensional guide no longer looked so alien-like, just from another time, and I found that this was once again a reminder that signs and signals are with us when we least expect it.

## A Message from the Angels

*When you open your heart, you let in light*

*When you allow light, you begin to feel at peace*

*When you feel peace, your heart is able to expand its capacity*

*When you expand your capacity and continue to fill with light, you raise your frequency*

*When you raise your frequency, you move into a higher plane*

*When you move into this higher plane, you are able to access more energy and remain in peace*

*When you access more energy, your heart expands, and the opening for creation and manifestation truly begins*

*and so it goes...*

—Laurie Wondra

# Connect with Your Loved Ones

Individuals often ask if they can connect with their loved ones directly. I tell them yes. Though I love when they come to see me, I want everyone to know that you can connect with your loved ones in various ways.

- **Letters**

The best way to connect with loved ones is to write a letter, or many letters, to them. The purpose is to tell them how you feel, and whatever else you want them to know or to answer for you. Write a letter; it can be one paragraph or eight pages, just write to them. Put the letter away, and wait for a period of time, which can be a week or two, but leave it be for a set period of time. After the time has passed, write another letter, this one being from your loved one to you. Don't worry about syntax, content, spelling, or grammar—just write. Write what comes to your mind or what comes through your pen. Just write and allow the words to flow onto the paper—with no right way or wrong way. Allow yourself the time and freedom to write.

Once you complete this writing, find the original letter that you wrote to your loved one. Read the entire letter. When finished with what you wrote to your loved one, read the letter you wrote that was from him/her to you. Do not be surprised at what was said to you in this letter, for your loved one answers. Some of my clients have told me stories of having totally forgotten what they had written in the first letter. Then they were shocked by the response they saw two weeks later when they read the letter they had written from their loved one to themselves. Given any chance, our loved ones want to connect to us; usually, the roadblock is that we do not pay attention to the messages they provide. Writing is the best way to help make this connection.

- **Dream State**

Another way to connect is to ask them to come to you in your dream state. You may ask this each night before you go to sleep, or keep a notepad by your bedside and write your request to them each night.

- **Meditation**

Meditation is another great way to connect. Some people find meditating difficult, but with practice, it does become easier. Meditation helps to remove yourself from right-brain thoughts and thought patterns, and move into a free space without any patterns. When we try too hard to meditate, we are remaining in that left-brain area. We become overly analytical with what we are supposed to be feeling or sensing, versus allowing ourselves to be in the right side of the brain and desensitizing our thoughts and feelings so we can just allow the messages to come to us. Sometimes meditating for a common connection may help. A loved one who is not as close to someone that has crossed over may get a response. This is because they are not trying as hard; rather, they are just allowing whatever message to come through. When we try too hard or focus too much, we create our own blockages. In meditation, be sure to breathe. Focusing on breathing will help you not focus on where the mind is trying to go. Let your mind and thoughts wander. Doing deep meditation, focusing on breathing, allows your vibration or frequency to rise, allowing you to be closer to the veil of the energies of those that have crossed over, and remain in those very high levels of energy. When we are on earth, we are in the third-dimensional energies, and when we cross over, we move within the higher levels, such as the fifth dimension. After loved ones cross, I suggest to clients to allow them time to become acclimated to their new energies. They need time to adjust before we pull them back down into the lower frequencies and vibrations.

The vibrations of this world are heavy and dense. I have had the heavenly frequencies described as light and airy. One man described that the freedom he felt after he left his body here on earth was like being catapulted from his heavy earthly body to feathers. He did not want to return to the heavy lower energies, and he wished that we all could understand this feeling of lightness.

As mentioned in earlier chapters, our loved ones often contact us through simple events. This may be a song, a scent, a breeze of air, or an animal. They *want* us to pay attention, and often work very hard to get our attention. As a teenager, I hated attending wakes held prior to the mass or funeral. It is done either the evening before or a few hours prior to the funeral. This allows loved ones to say their final good-byes, and friends and relatives to give their condolences to the person's family. I would often sit quietly and watch where the energy of the person that had passed would go, where it would linger, and where it would quickly pass. The energy would acknowledge all, and the love that I would feel would be immense. These energies work very hard to gain the attention of those that have come to say good-bye, and acknowledge everyone who was there.

At my own mother's funeral, since I am the youngest, I sat behind all my siblings. My daughter sat with me; my son had gone home ill with his father. I watched as my mother went to all in our family, lingered with each member, and bestowed her love on him/her. I have quite a large family, but she did not miss anyone. It felt as if time stood still as she spent time with each of us.

When she got to me, I could feel her touch my shoulder, and then I felt the rush of love pour over me. I leaned over to my daughter and whispered, "Did you feel that?" Her tears were an answer in themselves, and she simply nodded yes to my question.

At a recent circle, I led that group through a meditation where we connected and anchored our energy field to the elements below the surface of the earth. We then moved upward to a higher frequency to connect with the angelic realms. When we were done, I told the group to open their eyes when they were ready, and suggested they take time and allow themselves to see, hear, or feel whatever messages they were open to. There were tears in the room as a few asked if their loved ones had been present. They felt they had been basking in their love. Sometimes we forget to just be quiet and feel their love, their hugs, and their energy.

We are more connected to those that have crossed over than we realize; however, we must shift how we think of them. They have transitioned into another frequency plane and we have not, but our energies and the frequency of love keep us connected. We miss them in this plane, but we have access to them in their plane.

# Chapter 13

# Tell Them...

Sometimes, changes in our lives make us feel that we have lost control in places we never had control. This is only a reminder to trust that you'll have a path and a map.

Sometimes, we forget to take a step and find a bigger energy has shoved us as a means to get us moving because we have much more to do in this lifetime than to stand idle.

Sometimes, we are so crazy busy that we do not realize all the love we have available to us until we need help and see all the hands raised to help us, and we did not even ask.

*Sometimes, we want to cry and do not understand where the emotion is coming from because our left brains tell us it has to be from something. Be still. What you are feeling are the hugs and the love showered on you by your loved ones that have crossed. What they are telling you is that they love you forever.*

*Have gratitude for all those you love, have loved, and will yet love. Remember to tell them you appreciate and love them—unconditionally.*

When my clients ask me at a reading to give their loved one a message, I tell them to do it directly. They love when we continue to speak to them. As always, I tell my clients to write out their questions and list whom they would like to speak with prior to their appointment. Though I never look at their notes, their loved ones are often the first to speak up during a reading.

Katrina was very close to her grandfather, and as she and her sisters sat in my living room, ready for me to explain the process, I was immediately stopped by this loving man. He was so excited to be able to make this connection with his granddaughters. I watched his energy move from granddaughter to granddaughter until he settled in the middle of the room, feeling this was the place he most wanted to be—just like when he was alive. He was the center of a large, loving family, and he loved being surrounded by all his loved ones. He loved that he could remember their names—or at least most of them. He needed more time for some of the younger ones, and sometimes even a hint. He loved that he would be sought out for advice, and they would actually listen. He felt loved, respected, and at peace. He asked the three granddaughters which one had wanted to speak to him. Katrina did, because she again wanted his advice, and was hoping he would give it to her. She was making some life decisions, and his message to her was to simply be happy. He indicated that her other concerns about the family—some would work themselves out; some would not, but that was their "thorn." I did not know what this meant, but Katrina did.

Her grandfather often used the word *thorn* to describe something that was painful, and whatever was happening in her family at that time was certainly the thorn. Deep down she'd known this would be his response, and his use of the word *thorn* helped her validate what she had already known. Katrina asked me to thank her grandfather for always being there with all the right advice. He responded that although he liked this process of me channeling, he wished she would continue to talk to him directly.

Katrina explained to me that she believes she can talk to her grandfather, and if she listens closely, she believes she can almost recall how his words sounded, the tone of his voice, and his laughter. Still, the affirmation and confirmation is so comforting. It's the use of the word *thorn* that confirmed he was speaking. I asked her if she felt her grandfather near her often. He had shared that during his life he enjoyed being at the center of the family, and often liked being in the middle of everything. Now he was enjoying having a bird's-eye view. At that time, he was standing right next to her, and remained there until we were done with all three sisters' readings. As I hugged them good-bye, Katrina told me that she was grateful. She'd not only heard her grandfather, but had felt his presence near her until the time that we had finished. She said she often felt this same feeling, but didn't know it was him. That evening, it was validation in both hearing his words and feeling his presence that solidified for her that there still was a deep connection that would never be broken. As the three women walked down the sidewalk, Katrina yelled to the sky, "I love you, Grandpa!"

I coach people to stop second-guessing when they believe they are hearing or feeling their loved one with them. Sometimes their messages are very clear, as in Katrina's message from her grandfather, and sometimes they are not so clear.

On Valentine's Day, when I had committed to write for an hour, I received an urging from my own angels and guides that they wanted to speak about love. What better day to do this than when a large portion of the population was focused on love and feelings of the heart? As I sat down to write, I asked my angels and guides what messages they would like to share about love. I also wanted to know why they chose this day, when in my own belief system I felt that love should be given and shown on *all* days of the year. In some cases, I felt this day had become commercial, and perhaps from a place of obligation rather than from the heart.

After an hour of writing, answers to my "heart" questions began to come to me from my loved ones, angels, and guides, as well as from many elders of the universe.

Tell them: you are loved. Love is a universal emotion that travels planes and vibrational frequencies. It is infinite, and its reaches go well beyond what we experience, or what we allow ourselves to experience. It is all words and it is no words; it is the deep feeling of peace and belonging and being in sheer bliss. *Crazy love* is the term I kept hearing over and over again. It is that vibrational frequency that is so highly elevated that it connects us beyond our physical shape and our physical bodies. It continues beyond what we experience here in this earthly plane and in this frequency. Its vibrational experiences shape us, and the feelings that we have transform us. Its depth can never be removed, forgotten, or replaced, because it imprints within us. Though our loved ones leave this plane, that imprint and the connection of this frequency never break. Love is an energy that exists for us, and although forever changing, shifting, and growing, we remain connected. We have to be aware and believe that the connection is always available.

This means our loved ones are never far from us. We only have to see, feel, and sense their energy in another way, and at this higher frequency. We miss the physical presence and touch. We miss their voices, their laughter, and all things we remember from a physical plane. They want us to know that they continue to speak, to laugh, and to love. They have not stopped loving us. Why should we stop loving them?

The messages below are those that I most frequently hear, channel, and pass on to people that visit me.

*Tell them how much we love them*

*Tell them we are at peace*

*Tell them we are healed*

*Tell them we miss them*

*Tell them we are happy*

*Tell them we have not forgotten anyone*

*Tell them we are still connected*

*Tell them we see them*

*Tell them that we are very much a part of their lives*

*Tell them we see and watch over them*

*Tell them not to be afraid*

*Tell them to be happy and focus on living in joy*

*Tell them it is more beautiful here than they can imagine*

*Tell them we can't wait to one day share what we are experiencing and learning*

*Tell them that we will be together again one day*

—Laurie Wondra

# Chapter 14

# Last Messages

*Until we meet again, may our hearts and our souls remain connected in the highest place there exists. In the place of love. There are no last messages, as we communicate forever, albeit in a new method, a method some of us are not yet familiar with. May our connections forever bring us peace, joy, happiness, and the understanding that we will see each other again in a way that all is understood. Be at peace, and carry the torch of love forever in your heart.*

—Message from our loving angels that guide, protect, and love us

Sometimes the dying person's last messages are not heard, or there's been no opportunity to share any last messages. We know at some point that our loved ones will leave, or we will leave this plane, yet, due to circumstances, the last communication was not what you wanted it to be. You thought you had more time, you wanted to say more, or perhaps you wished you would have said less—not what we would want as our last words.

In the many years of seeing clients, I am most impacted by those clients that have found me in unique ways, or have been led to me to seek out answers. They may be seeking answers to help them bring closure to relationships or endings in a relationship, or to understand and gain information about what happened to their loved ones. This desire to know allows them to bring closure to the unknowns in their life. This is what brings people to my door most often. I marvel at how they found me, but I fully understand that they also have been led to me by loved ones. They may not hear all the information they are longing to hear. They may not find the answers they are seeking. But if it is meant to be, that they can bring some closure to events or relationships, or if they are able to create openings for a continuation of a relationship, and if a soul or heart healing is involved, the angels step in to assist.

Many times, experiences I have with clients linger with me. I find myself thinking about the impact people have on each other, and how important communication is. It is difficult to bring closure to a relationship when they are yet in this world, but it is even more difficult when they have left it, or if it is unknown that they have left this world. Many times I am unable to release the energy that the client may be feeling, and it takes time and focus to move this energy from a place of hurting to a place of healing. I am often in the middle of the energy exchange that happens between those sitting in my office and those that have crossed over. At times I try to remove myself from this energy field, and all I can do is ask the angels to be involved; to step in and take away the hurt or pain that may yet linger.

I often see the energy shift in these clients, which they experience from the time of the beginning of their reading when I meet them at my door, to the time of the end of their reading where I give them a hug to send them on their way. It is the awareness of their own emotions, and the deep desire that they hold to seek answers.

- This may be a young woman who, after almost ten years of searching, is seeking answers to where her father is, where he went, and what happened to him.

- A wife that would like to tell her husband she is sorry for the fight they had right before he went to the bedroom, where she later found him on the floor as the result of a sudden heart attack.

- For the person that left the room to answer the phone, and when she returned found her friend lifeless on the sofa. This left his family with the difficult decision of what to do, and unanswered questions as to what happened.

At some readings I am not able to provide all the specific information clients may be seeking, but if it is meant to be, they will hear what they need at that particular time to help comfort and bring closure. I depend on my guides and angels to help me, and help the client experience what he/she needs. Perhaps this particular time isn't right, but more often than not, their loved ones want to help bring answers, and often closure, when there has been a sudden passing.

In the case where the young man collapsed on the couch, though medical records showed it was a medical condition that caused his heart to stop, it left those behind wondering what they could have done differently in those minutes when his heart stopped. Did they get to him fast enough, did they wait too long, or could his life have been saved if other actions had been taken. The connection allows answers to those questions, and in this case, nothing could have been done. His journey ended as it had been planned. The healing messages came as the friends were able to reconnect and release the guilty feelings that they had not done enough. They were able to release the pain caused by simply not knowing what had happened to him. It was hard for these young friends to have their friend beside them one moment and gone the next, leaving them wondering where he went, and why he left so suddenly.

We often think that we have more control over life situations, such as this young man's life that ended when a viral infection attacked his heart. His friend wanted to know if he was all right now, and if he or the others could have done anything differently at that time. His pain of not knowing the answers to these questions had impacted his life, including his ability to trust or allow anyone to get close to him. He was afraid that if he became too close to others, he might lose them also. We often forget that some events in our lives impact us so deeply that they have the capability of setting a new course or they deviate us from the course we were on. We must understand that, at times, this is our journey, and this was all a piece of that journey. We should not second-guess ourselves based on our fears and hold back from living a robust life, or we might miss some amazing opportunities. Our loved ones want us to continue with our lives and be happy.

Healing may happen as a result of releasing bad memories of those that have passed. Perhaps it is the release of anger, or an understanding of why memories were lost if a loved one suffered memory losses as a result of Alzheimer's. Those loved ones that have passed with Alzheimer's or dementia want their loved ones here to know that they have their minds, their memory, and their abilities back. They do not want to be remembered by those last moments of dementia. Such was the grandmother who loudly entered her granddaughter's session with me, only to tell me that she was nice now, and was no longer angry, and it felt wonderful that she was released from exerting those emotions over which she had no control. She was at peace, and she wanted her granddaughter to also be at peace. She was insistent in explaining to her granddaughter that because of dementia, she didn't know what she was doing. Though her granddaughter had fully understood what was happening to her grandmother as she aged, it was important that the grandmother have a chance to explain.

Our loved ones and our angels want us to be at peace, and they work hard to bring that peace to allow the emotional healing to happen. Sometimes, the messages I hear are so difficult, and I find myself asking the angels to provide validation for the person that is with me. I ask if the person sitting in my office is ready to hear, and if so, to please provide him/her with additional angels and energy to be there to assist and support him/her. Such was the young woman that nervously sat in my office waiting to hear what she said she had already suspected, which was that her father had indeed passed many years ago, even though they continued to search for him. She was looking for validation to her own intuitive feelings. Yes, he had passed. As she walked into my office, her grandfather made his presence known. Although she said she'd barely known him, he knew her, and he was standing firm in being present for her. I sensed the messages were going to be immensely impacting in her life, but perhaps a painful necessity in the healing process. She was ready.

It was not by chance that she was sitting in my office. All had been coordinated very well for her to be there that day, including a cancellation that allowed her to move into that time slot for her reading. The angels were assisting—and this young woman was ready. Her grandfather was delivering the message that her father was there with him. I could not yet pick up the father's energy because he was hiding; embarrassed, guilty, and remorseful, with his head down. He was afraid he would not be loved and accepted for the choices he had made, and for the way his life had transpired. He had left his family, totally disappearing, but he was ready to face the emotions moving outward from his daughter. He had simply vanished and now here he was, beginning to see the pain he had brought to his family. As this young woman began to sob, he was feeling the total impact of her pain and her release of that pain. It was not hatred. In fact, it was the farthest thing from hatred; it was love. It was the wanting to know what happened and having the ability to say that, and know it had been delivered and heard, versus simply yelling it to the heavens. He was hearing her, and she was telling him directly.

When she left my office, she asked when she could return to again speak to her father, hoping he'd be farther along his healing journey and be able to speak with her. The angels told her to give him time. He had work to do, even though she had assisted in helping him move forward. I told her also to pay attention to her own intuition and her emotions, and understanding of the information he would be providing to her. A lot of information was given to her that day, and both she and he needed time to think and be in their own feelings about what they had both learned. Time does not heal all wounds. Understanding, information, and closure help us move along the road of healing, but when we love someone so deeply, it will never be erased, and it is unrealistic to believe that it would be. Time heals, but love heals deeper and faster, and our loved ones want us to feel their love.

Other times we might not have spoken to our loved ones in a very long time, as was the case where a woman's son had died. Entering my office, she almost fell into my arms, sobbing. She had nearly forgotten the sound of her son's voice, the pitch of his laughter. She didn't want to forget, and was struggling with holding on not only to the feeling of him being with her, but also to the sound and smells of him. She wanted to hold firm all the memories about him. She feared that the inability to remember his voice meant she was forgetting him. She did not want to forget him. I see many clients that keep phone messages or recorded messages from a loved one that has passed, simply to remember the sound of his/her voice. This young mother was no different in her desire to maintain that memory of her son.

Her son came to her, and I channeled his words—words that she would understand and that would comfort her—but it was my tone, not his. There was not a way for him to provide that memory to her, and so he simply provided words, and the feeling that he was hugging her. That was all he could offer, and he hoped it would be enough. He did not want his mom to be in such pain, and he hoped that the love they had felt for each other would sustain her in what she needed to remember him. His words were there, and his love would be there, too.

That first time Sondra, my administrative assistant, walked into my office with her father behind her, I knew he had a message for her. The difficult decision for me was whether I wanted anyone to know what I saw or felt. There was safety in not sharing any messages, and I didn't have to answer any questions about my gift. However, sometimes our loved ones are so very persistent that we cannot avoid or ignore that they are trying to reach out. Each subsequent time she came to my office, her father would follow. I was never afraid; I would only feel his energy, and see the smile that was there for her. He would bestow upon her his love to the point she'd almost appear as if she were glowing. I knew that at some point I would not be able to avoid telling her about my secret, and I trusted the angels would help me.

I'm not sure how I started the conversation one day, but her tears flowed as she listened to my words. His words to her were succinct in areas she would understand. I also then understood the importance of his words for her, and how they helped bring the feeling of peace that all would be OK with her mother. Sondra was at peace also knowing that her father would be waiting for her mother when she passed. When her terminally ill mother passed, she was met by Sondra's father, who had waited many years and was there to help her.

Months later, I met with Sondra, as she wanted to talk to her mother. Sondra needed to know that she had done everything her mother had hoped for after her crossing. She also wanted to know that her mom and dad were together, and that her mother had recovered from her illness. Knowing this allowed Sondra to be at peace. Though she missed them both very deeply, she found comfort and peace knowing her mother was well on her way to healing after spending the last few years of her life immobile and only able to speak in her native language, which few around her understood. Now she was surrounded by loved ones, angels, and the loveliest light beings—and she had many messages for Sondra.

When my own mother fell into a cancer-induced coma, I was on a business trip and vacation to Brazil and Argentina. When we landed in Sao Paulo, I instinctively looked at my phone. I had missed a call from my dad. It was very early in the morning, but without paying any attention to where I stood on the planet, and where he was at that time, I called him. I woke up both he and my mom. I apologized, but upon learning that I was standing at the airport in Brazil, they both wanted to speak to me. Neither had called me, but both were happy to talk to me. I didn't know it at that time, but this was the last time I would hear my mother's voice. Later in the week my older sister called, telling me Mother had an episode in the middle of the night, and they were now doing tests and brain scans. They found lesions on her brain, and later took a brain biopsy to see if it was cancer. A year earlier she had a similar event when in Florida, and my brother and I flew there to escort Mom and Dad home. We thought this might be a related event. The remainder of that trip was a blur, and she was deep in my thoughts, but communication back to the states was difficult. We were staying in a mountain villa that had electricity only in the kitchen; all other rooms and areas of the villa used candles and wood-burning fireplaces. We had to drive to town for Internet or cell phone reception. I debated getting on a plane and coming home or waiting until my planned return later that week. Taking everything into consideration, I completed my trip and flew home, knowing that her spirit was already in the process of preparing for death. I had many etheric conversations with her even while out of the country.

Mom never regained consciousness, and I next saw her in the hospice as her body withered. This was not how she wanted any of us to remember her.

She was a woman that enjoyed life and exploring while traveling all over the United States. Her sense of adventure and exploration has not stopped; she is now doing it on a different plane. Her love of gardens, flowers, and being outside is a legacy she has left behind with her children, and every now and then I smell the scent of fresh-cut flowers, even though I may not have any in my home. This is her way to remind me that she is still very much a part of my life, but it's also a reminder to enjoy the outdoors.

When I was in Argentina, we spent a day hiking to the top of Cerro Uritorco, a mountain (*cerro*) and the highest peak of the Sierras Chicas chain in the northwest of the province of Córdoba. The elevation is 1,949 meters, or 6,394 feet, and it takes three to four hours for the hike up, and signs tell you it will take three hours to hike down. Atop this mountain are the most amazing views of Calabalumba River, and a cross that visitors often tie messages and notes to that speak to their loved ones. It feels as if you are meeting the point where this plane touches the heavenly realms. Before our descent, we spent quiet time meditating and journaling. I left a message to my mother there, telling her how deeply I loved her, and that all would be fine here on earth. I knew she would continue to watch over all of us and envelop us with her love. On the top of this mountain, I felt touched by heaven.

During the hike down, I took many photos, and some of them contain lovely huge orbs that to this day I believe are the angels and energy beings that assist hikers on that mountain. During my meditation and journaling atop the mountain, I received many messages of affirmation that love never stops, never fades, and it certainly never dies. The memories and feelings that we have for our loved ones while they are here on earth continue to grow and transform. I also believe that, in some way, my mother's energy was with me as I sat on the rocks of that mountaintop. Though unable to hike and venture out to such a place for many, many years, she still always enjoyed nature. I know her adventure continues now, and she is exploring just as she did when she was here on earth. I know she, and all our loved ones, is experiencing the rainbows that are more colorful and vibrant than words can describe. Sunsets and sunrises are unbelievably beautiful in both their colors and the energy that comes with those moments. Life as they know it is more peaceful and fulfilling.

A number of years ago, I was honored to be sitting with a man as he waited to transition into the next phase of his journey. He knew he was dying, and all he could do was wait. He was a shaman, an intuitive, a healer, a teacher, and some would call him an Ascended Master. I had felt that he would be leaving this earth that year, but when the phone call came to me in Minnesota that he had been taken to the hospital, and then to hospice, it was still difficult to hear that he was near the end. I made the trip to see him, not knowing what to expect. After landing at the airport, I drove straight to the hospice. When I arrived, the administration was going over paperwork with him—paperwork that stated he would be declining any life support or other treatment. I knew this was his wish, based on phone conversations with both him and those closer to him. I waited patiently in the hall as the administrator spoke to him. I could hear my friend answer yes to the questions. I also heard him explain that he thought all had been decided, and had already been taken care of that morning, so he didn't understand the formality of what they were doing or all the paperwork for someone who was dying. I don't think he had spent any time in a hospital in his life, so all this must have felt very foreign. The administrator motioned for me to come into the room. My friend continued to ask the administrator if all the paperwork truly mattered. I could see on his face that he continued to ponder this, even as the administrator verified that they had to have all their documentation in order. I pulled a chair up near the bed and sat, taking my friend's hand in mine. I listened as he recalled the events that led up to this time. He was very alert and was thinking clearly, but his body had given out and begun to shut down. As we simply talked about things, the administrator came back and asked my friend for his signature on the all the paperwork. Then he asked me to witness him signing these papers. My friend started laughing, and began to talk about the importance of being the witness. He marveled at the timing of my arrival. It hadn't been yesterday, or that morning, or even that evening, it had been at that exact time—and my purpose of being there was to witness. Now he seemed to understand the importance of all the paperwork—not from the standpoint of the law or the state's requirements, but simply from the law of the universe. Let it be witnessed, he was ready. He said that he had been ready for a while, and he continued to ponder the significance of this, which did nothing to make me feel any more comfortable about the timing of my arrival and my participation in these events.

When I asked him what I could do, he said he would like to meditate with me. So I sat holding his hand, and allowed myself to go where the angels wanted to take me. I believed I was there for him and his friend who was not able to be there, but his gift to me was my surprise. I am not sure how long we sat this way, but when I opened my eyes, my friend was staring at me. He asked me what I had seen. In other words, he was asking me if I had seen the same thing he did. I explained I had been taken higher through the levels of knowledge until I came upon a field. He had been standing in the middle of this field, and as time went on, others came to sit in a circle around him. They were coming to listen to him, and he was teaching and preparing them, telling them stories and giving lessons. He was dressed in the clothing of a shaman, a master, or an elder of the tribe, and he held his staff as he spoke to all that were coming to him.

I told him how the colors were indescribable. When I wanted to look more closely, the brightness of the light and colors made me look away. I tried to see who was around his circle, but was not allowed. I only knew that they were there to learn from him, and he was preparing them for some journey on which they were about to embark. I felt his energy and that of those around the circle, and felt at total peace. I could feel the love that was showering down on him, and outward to the circle of people now seated all around him. As he was teaching, others behind him were teaching him; he was learning and teaching. And with the synergy in this process was balance in the give-and-take and the ebb and flow of the energy. Though I felt that he was in the middle of this group, I also felt there were other groups, and these groups were in the middle of something larger and broader that was supporting him. To this day, that field is vividly locked in my mind. Then the light shifted and became stars, and though the brightness of the energy shifted and faded, the intensity of the energy did not diminish. My meditation stopped when I saw him begin to walk away, toward a backdrop of beautiful lights, like a lovely sunset or the northern lights. I did not have the words to describe it. I heard him say yes; simply yes, like he was in agreement with this. "It was beautiful, wasn't it?" were his next words. I asked him what he was experiencing, and he said that he was at peace. He was simply told to wait. He was waiting for all the information to be given to him as part of preparing for his journey. I asked him if he was scared, and he said no, because he had done this before, and it was just a matter of waiting. When the time was right he would be ready; he just needed to be patient. He didn't know what he needed to "do" yet, but believed that when he dozed off, they were providing him with information, preparing him. He felt very much at peace.

The next time I saw my friend, he was farther along on his journey and was sleeping or dozing more. He was heavily medicated. Again I held his hand. He asked me why I had come, and I told him that I had promised to be back, and had brought a mutual friend with me to visit. Both were healers, very gifted intuitive people. I left the room to allow them to talk, and as I walked down the hall, I could hear the words of my ill friend, teaching, sharing, and in awe of where he was.

My friend passed shortly after that. I know he is very much at peace, and is already busy in the etheric planes. I hear from mutual friends that he still reaches out to them with messages and helpful information. He is not gone. He reminds us that he has only transformed, and if we listen we can hear him.

This year, the day before my mother's birthday was a Friday, and it was going to be a long weekend. I'd slept restlessly that night, and at 6:08 a.m. that Friday, the house phone rang. The caller ID said Virginia, Minnesota. As I reached to answer it, it stopped ringing. When I looked again, there was no phone number, it simply said Virginia, Minnesota. I do not know anyone in Virginia, Minnesota, but I quickly realized it was the day before my mom's birthday, and her first name is Virginia. I laughed. It was like her to urge us to get out of bed and not waste the day away. On this morning, she obviously wanted me awake prior to my alarm.

The next day was a Saturday, and after a restless night, I was at my home office desk by seven fifteen that morning. At seven thirty, I heard an alarm go off somewhere in the basement. The kids were upstairs in their rooms still sleeping, and no "extra" teens were sleeping over that day. I tracked the alarm to an atomic clock in the basement that we never knew even had an alarm to set. As I picked up the clock to look for a place to shut off the alarm, it stopped on its own. To this day, we are mystified as to who set it, and how it went off *only* on that day—*my mom's birthday*. I wished her a happy birthday, sent her love, and sat on the couch with the clock cradled in my lap, allowing myself to connect to her energy.

So it is with our loved ones. They do not leave us. They leave their bodies behind and move to an etheric plane of energy where they are allowed to live more freely. They have left behind their physical and/ or emotional pain, and are now in the midst of deep love and joy. They remind us that someday we will be joined with them again, and at that time we can also experience what they are experiencing—deep love, deep joy, and deep happiness.

# Chapter 15

# The Next Chapter

The world, as we think we know it, is ever changing, and the simple fact that you are reading this book means that *you* (and all people) are also forever changing. The next chapter means "a continuation" of our evolution.

Would it not be logical, then, to think that those who have left this earth continue on in some form? Some might say:

- They have lived a full life, insinuating that once we leave this planet, we are done.

- When we leave this planet, we do not return.

- We can live again and again and again through a reincarnation process.

I've met skeptical people who want to test anyone's ability to communicate with or experience things that cannot be seen, heard, or touched. Whatever our belief system is, it supports how we experience our life and how we experienced the stories in this book. If we are rigid in our belief system, we may limit what we are able to experience. I learned as a young teen to let go of what I thought I knew, and I most definitely needed to let go of what I believed about death. There were times in my life when I felt I had no solid beliefs about death, and I struggled defining what, exactly, is the dying process, and what exists beyond death. I felt the information was forever changing, and often found myself desperately wanting to share what I experienced. I wanted to tell others what I was seeing and feeling, so they could help me explain what, exactly, was this thing called "the afterlife." I wanted someone to tell me the experiences were real—and not my imagination. I couldn't explain why I would tear up when a person would tell me about someone in his/her life who had died. I could sense the energy of the dead person, but I was petrified to say anything. Would anyone believe me? Through these experiences with the dead and the living, I realized the information was not changing; rather, I was learning, and with each client and each session with the angels and guides, they were teaching me, and therefore my belief system was adjusting.

As I continue to work with angels and energy beings, I've learned that what we know is not a fixed entity. When we open ourselves to any experience, we continue the educational process—and that never ends. The brain has an amazing capacity, but the soul is limitless in its capacity. As a child, and later as a young woman, I never dreamed I would be speaking to angels, guides, and dead people, and then later writing about those experiences. Many of my clients also didn't believe they would ever connect with those who had died until they themselves also passed. They let go of any apprehension, let go of any beliefs that created a roadblock, and in the process experienced a reconnect, a healing, and they did in fact hear the messages their loved ones wanted them to hear.

It's very true that when working with a client, I have to listen extremely carefully, and pass on that message to my client. Her job is to listen and try to determine what the message means. Sometimes the message doesn't become clear until later, as time passes and the perspective changes. Sometimes they come to hear one message, and hear another—the one the guides and angels of their loved ones want them to hear because they *know* that is what they need to hear.

As I've said many times, most of us want to know that the loved one who passed is happy, and in a good place, and, just as important, that he/she is full of love for those left behind. All else doesn't matter.

What an exciting and affirming role I have, passing on the messages of love, forgiveness, acceptance, and so on from those who have passed to those waiting to learn that, in truth, they were and still are loved. I am deeply grateful for this gift I have been graced with.

17769107R00085

Made in the USA
Charleston, SC
27 February 2013